JUST

COCKTAILS

TOP THAT!™

Copyright © 2005 Top That! Publishing Inc
25031 W. Avenue Stanford,
Suite #60, Valencia
CA 91355
www.topthatpublishing.com

Introduction

The history of the cocktail is somewhat blurred. All that can be said for certain is that mixed drinks, both alcoholic and non-alcoholic have been drunk throughout the world for hundreds of years

Predictably, claims for the origin of the word "cocktail" are accompanied by colourful and outlandish anecdotes. A popular story is that of Betsy Flanagan, an innkeeper during the American War of Independence. She is said to have served American and French officers a meal of roast chicken, stolen from a nearby English farmer. The officers washed down their meal with drinks decorated with the bird's tail feathers, mocking their enemy with toasts of "vive le cocktail!"

Another story tells of an American bar, where a large ceramic container in the shape of a cockerel was used to store the leftovers of drinks. The potent, if sometimes unpalatable mixture, was served from a

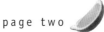

tap at the "tail" of the bird, hence the term "cocktail." Other theories are based upon anything from drunken fighting cocks to docked horse's tails—every cocktail aficionado will have their favorite story.

The Martini is generally agreed to be the first modern cocktail. The classic mix of gin and vermouth, garnished with a cherry or olive was popular across the USA by 1900. However, mixed drinks really took off during prohibition in the USA. The illegal hooch produced by the bootleggers generally tasted awful, so recipes were concocted to make it more palatable. Cocktail favorites such as the Harvey Wallbanger and the Manhattan all date from this time.

The classic cocktail conjures up images of style and sophistication, cool and glamour. Exotic-tasting mixes remind us of holidays, frivolity, fun, and even danger. So try the recipes in this book and realize your own cocktail fantasy!

 page three

Equipment

Making quality cocktails requires a range of special bar equipment. The cocktail shaker is essential. Your need for the other items will depend on the type of drinks you make the most and whether or not you are a stickler for detail

Bar spoon

Long-handled spoons used mainly for mixing drinks directly in the glass. Also used for "muddling"—crushing sugar, herbs or other ingredients

Blender

Used for blending frothy cocktails or mixing in crushed ice. The tall, goblet style blenders are best for cocktails

Cocktail shaker

The three-piece shaker has a base to hold ice and a built-in strainer. The larger Boston shaker can mix drinks more quickly, but you will need a separate strainer

Corkscrew/bottle opener
No bar would be complete without this

Fruit squeezer
Freshly-squeezed fruit juices are essential for certain cocktails

Measures
These are essential for measuring the right amount of alcohol—one measure is roughly equivalent to one tablespoon

Mixing glass
A large glass beaker used to stir cocktails

Nutmeg grater
Does exactly what it says. Grates nutmeg very finely to top off Eggnogs and other frothy drinks

Strainer
Used with a Boston shaker to separate the pips and fruit pulp from the drink

Ice crusher
Used for crushing ice. Specialist mechanical and electric ice crushers are also available

Glasses

Good presentation is very much a part of enjoying cocktails. For some, only the correct glass will do, but you should use whatever you think looks good

(1) Champagne glass
The old-fashioned bowl is a very elegant and stylish way to serve Champagne or Champagne cocktails. However, the flute helps to preserve the fizz

(2) Highball/Collins glass
Tall tumblers used to serve long, ice-filled drinks with soda or fruit juice. The Collins is slightly larger than the highball

(3) Cocktail/Martini glass
This is the classic symbol of cocktail culture. Elegant, cool, and sophisticated, the conical bowl on a tall stem is traditionally used for Martinis

(3)

(1)

(4) Tumbler/rocks glass
Short, sturdy glasses used for serving drinks over ice, or "on the rocks"

(5) Shot glass
Very small glass used for consuming (or measuring) shots of spirit

(6) Wine glasses
Various sizes are useful for wine and different types of cocktails. Long stems help to keep warm hands away from your chilled drink

(5)

Techniques

Crushing ice

Many cocktails use crushed ice or "ice snow" as an ingredient. You must crush ice before using it in a blender

(1) Place a tea towel on a worktop and partly cover it with ice cubes. Fold the cloth over the cubes

(2) Using an ice crusher, hit the ice firmly to crush it

(3) Spoon the ice pieces into your glasses, blender, or mixing jug. Large pieces can be stored in bags in the freezer, but the fine "ice snow" must be used immediately

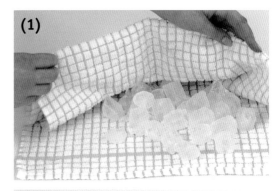

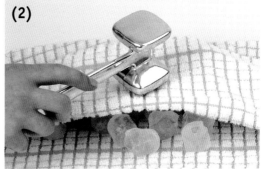

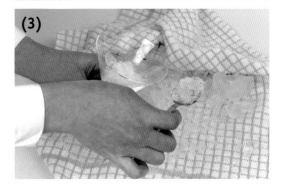

Frosted glasses

Many types of cocktails are enhanced by being served in a glass with a frosted rim. Salt or sugar are typically used, but you could create your own

(1) Holding the glass upside down, rub the rim with the cut surface of a lemon, orange or other suitable fruit

(2) Dip the rim in a shallow layer of the sugar or salt. Make sure the rim is well coated

(3) Leave the glass upright until the rim is dry. Chill in the fridge if necessary

Essentials and Tips

Flavorings
Essential cocktail flavorings include hot pepper sauce, Worcestershire sauce, and Angostura bitters

Garnishes
Colorful and tasty garnishes can really make a difference to a cocktail. They should be fresh and of good quality. Cherries, lemons, limes, and pineapples are common for sweet drinks; drier tastes may be finished with olives, celery or onions

Glasses
Make sure glasses are washed, dried, and very clean. Never serve a cocktail in a warm glass—chill it in the refrigerator if necessary

Ice
Do not be afraid to use lots of ice. It keeps the drink cooler for a lot longer

Measures

An extra-large measure of alcohol does not improve a cocktail. Keep to the amounts shown in the recipes for reasons of class and authenticity. If you need more alcohol, mix up another cocktail!

Mixers

Always use the best mixers that you can afford. For juices, fresh is definitely best and make sure creams are not past their best. Some essential mixers include: cranberry, lemon, orange, lime, tomato and pineapple juices, cola, and tonic water

Sweeteners

Superfine sugar mixes into drinks well or even better make, or buy, some sugar syrup

Twist or slice?

A twist is a small strip of lemon or lime peel. Squeezing the twist over the drink will release the oils from the peel. Do not make slices too thick or thin

Contents

Applesinthe

Glass: Highball

Ingredients:
Two measures of absinthe
Half a teaspoon of gomme syrup
One teaspoon of passion syrup
Two measures of fresh lemon juice
One measure of apple schnapps
Four measures of fresh apple juice
Dash of orange bitters

Method:
Shake ingredients and strain over crushed ice into a highball

Garnish:
With slices or wedges of apple

B-52

Glass: Tumbler

Ingredients:
One measure of chocolate liqueur
One measure of Irish cream liqueur
One measure of cognac-based
orange liqueur

Method:
Shake the ingredients together and pour over ice into a tumbler glass. Can also be served as a shooter.

Between the Sheets

Glass: Cocktail

Ingredients:
Two measures of brandy
Two measures of orange liqueur
Two measures of white rum
One measure of fresh lemon juice

Method:
Shake ingredients with ice and strain into a chilled cocktail glass

Garnish:
With a long lemon zest twist

Black Russian*

Glass: Tumbler

Ingredients:
Four measures of vodka
Two measures of chocolate liqueur

Method:
Pour the ingredients over ice into a
tumbler glass

Garnish:
With cherries

*You can turn the Black Russian into a
Long Black Russian by changing the
glass to a highball and topping
the drink with cola*

Black Velvet

Glass: Wine

Ingredients:
Champagne
Irish stout

Method:
Half fill a wine glass with the Irish stout and top up with Champagne

Blood & Sand

Glass: Cocktail

Ingredients:
Two measures of Scotch whisky
Two measures of cherry liqueur
Two measures of sweet vermouth
Two measures of fresh orange juice

Method:
Shake ingredients with ice and strain into a
chilled cocktail glass

Garnish:
With an orange slice

Bloody Mary

Glass: Highball

Ingredients:
Four measures of vodka
Sixteen measures of tomato juice
Freshly squeezed juice of a lemon
Pinch of salt and pepper
A few dashes of hot pepper sauce
Half a teaspoon of horseradish sauce
Four to six dashes of Worcestershire sauce
Pinch of celery salt

Method:
Shake all the ingredients together with a scoop of ice

Garnish:
Serve in a highball glass garnished with a lemon slice and a stick of celery

Blue Hawaiian

Glass: Wine

Ingredients:
Four measures of white rum
Two measures of blue Curaçao
Eight measures of pineapple juice
Four measures of cream of coconut
Crushed ice

Method:
Add ingredients to a blender and mix for 20-30 seconds, pour into a wine glass

Garnish:
With a pineapple wedge and a cocktail umbrella

Bucks Fizz*

Glass: Flute

Ingredients:
Four to eight measures of freshly-squeezed
orange juice
Champagne

Method:
Pour the orange juice into a flute and top
with chilled dry Champagne

Also known as the Mimosa

Caipirinha

Glass: Tumbler

Ingredients:
Four measures of cachaca
One lime
Two brown sugar cubes

Method:
Cut the lime into eights and place into a tumbler glass with the sugar cubes and swirl together. Fill the glass with crushed ice and top with cachaca and stir

Garnish:
With a wedge of lime

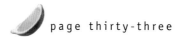

Champagne Cocktail*

Glass: Flute

Ingredients:
Two measures of brandy
One white sugar cube
Angostura bitters
Champagne

Method:
Cover the sugar cube in Angostura bitters and place into a flute. Add the brandy and top with Champagne

This Cocktail is also known as the Classic Champagne Cocktail and sometimes the Business Brace

Cosmopolitan

Glass: Cocktail

Ingredients:
Four measures of lemon vodka
Two measures of orange liqueur
Dash of cranberry juice
Squeeze of fresh lime

Method:
Shake and strain into a chilled cocktail glass

Garnish:
With flamed lime zest

Daiquiri (original)

Glass: Highball

Ingredients:
Four measures of golden rum
One measure of fresh lime juice
One measure of sugar syrup

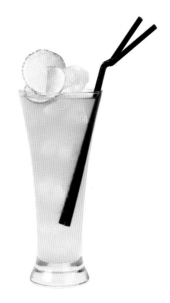

Method:
Shake with ice and strain into a
highball glass over fresh ice

Garnish:
With a twisted slice of lime or serve in a
sugar-frosted glass

Eggnog

Glass: Tumbler

Ingredients:
Two measures of brandy
Two measures of dark rum
One egg white
One teaspoon of sugar
Milk
Nutmeg

Method:
Shake all ingredients (except milk) with ice. Strain into a tumbler glass. Top up with milk

Garnish:
With a sprinkle of nutmeg

Fuzzy Navel

Glass: Tumbler

Ingredients:
Four measures of peach schnapps
Orange juice

Method:
Pour the peach schnapps over ice. Top up
with orange juice

Garnish:
With an orange slice

Gimlet

Glass: Cocktail

Ingredients:
Four measures of gin
Two measures of lime cordial
One lime wedge

Method:
Pour gin and lime cordial into a shaker with ice, squeeze in the lime juice and add the wedge. Shake and strain into a cocktail glass

Garnish:
With a slice of lime and a cherry or served in a frosted cocktail glass

Grasshopper

Glass: Cocktail

Ingredients:
Two measures of white crème de cacao
Two measures of green crème de menthe
Two measures of fresh cream

Method:
Shake ingredients vigorously and strain into a cocktail glass

Garnish:
With cherries and a sprig of mint

Harvey Wallbanger

Glass: Highball

Ingredients:
Four measures of vodka
One measure of galliano
Fresh orange juice

Method:
Into a highball filled with ice, pour the vodka, and orange juice. Then float the galliano on the top

Garnish:
With an orange slice

Hawaiian

Glass: Cocktail

Ingredients:
Four measures of gin
One measure of triple sec
One measure of pineapple juice

Method:
Shake all the ingredients together with some crushed ice. Strain and pour

Garnish:
With cherries and an orange slice

Income Tax

Glass: Tumbler

Ingredients:
Four measures of gin
One measure of dry vermouth
Two measures of orange juice
Two or three dashes of bitters

Method:
Shake all the ingredients with the crushed
ice. Strain and pour over fresh ice

Garnish:
With a slice of orange

Jamaican Slammer

Glass: Shot

Ingredients:
One measure of golden rum
One measure of triple sec
Five drops of lime
One measure of dark rum

Method:
Pour the dark rum into the shot glass. Next float the triple sec and then add the lime juice before floating the golden rum on top

John Collins

Glass: Highball

Ingredients:
Four measures of whisky
Two measures of lemon juice
Dash of sugar syrup
Soda water

Method:
Shake the whisky, lemon juice, and sugar syrup along with crushed ice. Strain and pour over more ice. Top up with soda water and stir gently

Garnish:
With orange and lemon segments and a cherry

Kir Royale

Glass: Flute

Ingredients:
One measure of crème de cassis
Champagne

Method:
Pour the cassis into a flute and top with
chilled Champagne

Long Island Iced Tea

Glass: Highball

Ingredients:
One measure of vodka
One measure of gin
One measure of white rum
One measure of tequila
One measure of triple sec
Two measures of fresh lemon juice
Dash of gomme syrup
Cola

Method:
Build ingredients over ice into a highball glass, top with cola

Garnish:
With a slice of lime

Mai Tai

Glass: Highball

Ingredients:
Four measures of rum
One measure of orange Curaçao
One measure of apricot brandy
One measure of fresh lime juice
One measure of pineapple juice
Dash of Angostura bitters
Two dashes of orgeat syrup

Method:
Shake all ingredients with ice and strain into an ice-filled highball glass

Garnish:
With a twist of orange

Manhattan

Glass: Cocktail

Ingredients:
Four measures of whisky
Two measures of sweet vermouth
Dash of bitters
A cherry to garnish

Method:
Stir together with ice, strain into a
cocktail glass

Garnish:
With a cherry

Margarita

Glass: Cocktail

Ingredients:
Two measures of gold tequila
Two measures of triple sec
Two measures of fresh lime juice

Method:
Frost the rim of the glass with salt. Shake all the ingredients with cracked ice. Strain and pour into the salt-frosted glass

Martini (dry)

Glass: Cocktail

Ingredients:
Four measures of gin
One measure of dry vermouth
Green olives or lemon zest

Method:
Pre-chill your glass, fill the mixing jug with ice, add the pre-chilled ingredients in the required ratios. Stir quickly and smoothly for approximately ten seconds and then pour into the chilled glass

Garnish:
Serve with olives or a strip of lemon zest

Metropolitan

Glass: Cocktail

Ingredients:
Four measures of brandy
Two measures of sweet vermouth
A dash of Angostura bitters

Method:
Coat the glass with the Angostura bitters.
Shake the brandy and vermouth with
cracked ice. Strain and pour into a chilled
cocktail glass

Garnish:
With a cherry

Mojito

Glass: Highball

Ingredients:
Four measures of light rum
Four white cane sugar cubes
(or dash of gomme syrup)
Seven or eight fresh mint leaves
A sliced and diced lime
Soda water

Method:
Muddle the mint, sugar, and lime in a highball, then fill the glass with crushed ice, pour the rum, top up with soda, and stir

Garnish:
With a sprig of mint and twist of lime

Moscow Mule

Glass: Highball

Ingredients:
Four measures of vodka
Two measures of fresh lime juice
Ginger beer

Method:
Build ingredients over ice into a
highball glass

Garnish:
With a wedge of lime

Nelson's Blood

Glass: Flute

Ingredients:
Two measures of ruby port
Champagne

Method:
Pour ingredients into a champagne flute

October Revolution

Glass: Highball

Ingredients:
Four measures of vodka
Four measures of coffee liqueur
Four measures of crème de cacao
Four measures of heavy cream

Method:
Shake ingredients with ice, strain into a
highball glass containing ice

Garnish:
Serve with a straw

Pina Colada

Glass: Highball

Ingredients:
Four measures of golden rum
Two measures of cream
Two measures of coconut milk
Four measures of pineapple juice

Method:
Shake ingredients with ice and strain over ice into a highball glass

Garnish:
With a pineapple wedge and a cocktail umbrella

Pink Gin

Glass: Tumbler

Ingredients:
Four measures of gin
Dash of Angostura bitters

Method:
Pour ingredients over ice into a tumbler
glass and stir to chill

Garnish:
Squeeze in oils from a lemon zest and use a
slice of lemon as garnish

Pink Lady*

Glass: Cocktail

Ingredients:
Two measures of gin
Two measures of orange liqueur
Two measures of fresh lemon juice
Dash of egg white (optional)
Dash of grenadine

Method:
Shake ingredients with ice and strain into a chilled cocktail glass

To change into a White Lady take out the dash of grenadine

Red, White & Blue

Glass: Shot

Ingredients:
One measure of grenadine
One measure of peach schnapps
One measure of blue Curaçao

Method:
Pour the grenadine. Next float the peach schnapps, then the blue Curaçao

This cocktail works better if you chill the ingredients beforehand

Rob Roy

Glass: Cocktail

Ingredients:
Three measures of Scotch whisky
Two measures of sweet vermouth
A dash of Angostura bitters

Method:
Add ingredients to an ice-filled mixing glass and stir until chilled. Strain into a cocktail glass

Garnish:
Garnish with lemon zest and a cherry

Make a Dry Rob Roy by replacing the sweet vermouth with a dry vermouth and make a perfect Rob Roy by using half sweet and half dry vermouths

Rusty Nail

Glass: Tumbler

Ingredients:
Two measures of whisky
Two measures of drambuie

Method:
Pour ingredients over ice into a
tumbler glass

Garnish:
With a slice of orange

Sea Breeze

Glass: Highball

Ingredients:
Four measures of vodka
Twelve measures of cranberry juice
Four measures of grapefruit juice

Method:
Build over ice into a highball glass

Garnish:
With a lime slice

Sex on the Beach

Glass: Highball

Ingredients:
Two measures of vodka
Two measures of peach schnapps
Twelve measures of fresh cranberry juice
Four measures of orange juice

Method:
Shake ingredients with ice and strain into a highball filled with fresh ice

Garnish:
With orange or lime slices

Singapore Sling

Glass: Tumbler

Ingredients:
Four measures of gin
Two measures of cherry brandy
A dash of sugar syrup
One measures of fresh lime juice
Soda water

Method:
Shake ingredients with ice and pour into a tumbler glass filled with ice. Top with soda water

Garnish:
With a slice of lime

Thin Blue Line

Glass: Shot

Ingredients:
One measure of of triple sec
One measure of of vodka
Four or five drops of blue Curaçao

Method:
Pour the triple sec and float the vodka carefully over the top of it. Then, with a straw or dropper, add the Curaçao drops

This cocktail works better if you chill the ingredients beforehand

Tokyo Silver Fizz

Glass: Highball

Ingredients:
Two measures of vodka
Two measures of melon liqueur
One measure of lemon juice
Dash of egg white
Soda water

Method:
Shake ingredients (except soda) and strain over fresh ice into a highball. Top with soda water

Garnish:
Top with a lemon slice

Vodkatini

Glass: Cocktail

Ingredients:
Four measures of vodka
A dash of dry vermouth

Method:
Stir the vermouth and vodka with ice in a pre-chilled mixing glass. Stir until chilled and strain into a chilled cocktail glass

Garnish:
With a pitted olive or lemon zest

Whisky Sour

Glass: Tumbler

Ingredients:
Four measures of whisky
Two measures of lemon juice
Two measures of sugar syrup

Method:
Mix the ingredients in a tumbler glass over ice

Garnish:
With a twist of lemon

White Russian

Glass: Tumbler

Ingredients:
Four measures of vodka
Two measures of chocolate liqueur
Two measures of single cream

Method:
Pour the vodka and the chocolate liqueur
into a tumbler glass filled with ice. Layer
the cream on top

Garnish:
With a stemmed cherry

Xantippe

Glass: Cocktail

Ingredients:
Four measures of vodka
Two measures of yellow chartreuse
Two measures of cherry brandy

Method:
Stir the ingredients vigorously with ice.
Strain into a chilled cocktail glass

Yellow Ribbon

Glass: Tumbler

Ingredients:
Four measures of mandarin vodka
Two measures of lemon juice
One measure of frangelico
One measure of gomme sugar syrup

Method:
Shake and strain into a tumbler glass

Garnish:
With a lemon wedge

Zombie

Glass: Highball

Ingredients:
Two measures of lemon juice
Two teaspoons of grenadine
Two dashes of Angostura bitters
Two measures of spiced rum
Ten measures of orange juice
Two measures of apricot brandy
Four measures of guava/mango/
other exotic juices
Two measures of light rum
One measure of "float" of dark rum

Method:
In a highball glass pour the ingredients
in order as above

Garnish:
With lemon and lime slices

Non-alcoholic cocktails

Non-alcoholic cocktails allow drivers, teetotallers and children to enjoy the suave indulgence of a cocktail, without the side effects that come with alcohol

Often vibrantly fruity and refreshing, and with equally exotic mixes of ingredients, you'll hardly notice the difference as you sample the delights of a Brown Horny Toad, a Honeymoon, or maybe a Starburst, that can be enjoyed any time of day, in any situation

Brown Horny Toad

Glass: Highball

Four measures of pineapple juice
Four measures of orange juice
Two measures of lemon juice
Dash of grenadine
Dash of gomme syrup
Pinch of ground cinnamon
Pinch of ground cloves

Method:
Shake ingredients with ice and strain over fresh ice into a highball

Garnish:
With an orange and lemon slice

Caribbean Cocktail

Glass: Tumbler

Ingredients:
Fresh mango (skinned)
A banana
Juice of an orange
A dash of fresh lime juice

Method:
Blend the mango and banana with the juices and a few ice cubes until smooth. Strain over fresh ice into a tumbler

Garnish:
With slices of banana and a cocktail umbrella

Honeymoon

Glass: Cocktail

Ingredients:
Two measures of clear honey
One measure of fresh lime juice
Two measures of orange juice
Two measures of apple juice

Method:
Shake ingredients with crushed ice and strain into a cocktail glass

Garnish:
With a cherry

San Francisco

Glass: Wine

Ingredients:
Two measures of fresh orange juice
Two measures of fresh lemon juice
Two measures of fresh pineapple juice
Two measures of fresh grapefruit juice
One measure of grenadine
A dash of egg white
Soda water

Method:
Shake ingredients (apart from the soda)
with ice, strain over fresh ice into a wine
glass, and top up with soda water

Garnish:
With lemon, lime, and orange slices

Starburst

Glass: Highball

Ingredients:
One banana
One kiwi
Ten fresh strawberries
Twelve measures of apple juice
Crushed ice

Method:
Slice fruit and place into a blender
with apple juice. After blending pour into a
highball

Garnish:
With strawberries

Glossary

All of the ingredients needed to make the cocktails in this book are listed

Absinthe
Infamous, very powerful spirit. Said to have hallucinogenic properties

Angostura bitters
Bitter flavoring derived from tree bark

Apple juice
Apple schnapps
Apricot brandy
Banana
Blackcurrant vodka
Vodka with a twist of blackcurrant

Blue Curaçao
Liqueur flavored with orange peel

Brandy
Cachaca
White Brazilian rum made from sugar cane

Celery
Celery salt
Champagne
Cherries
Cherry brandy
Chocolate dust
Powdered chocolate for garnishing

Coconut cream

Coffee liqueur

Cognac-based orange liqueur

Cola

Cranberry juice

Cream
Single and heavy

Cream of coconut

Crème de cacao
Brandy-based liqueur with cacao

Crème de cassis
Brandy-based liqueur with cherries

Crème de menthe
Brandy-based liqueur with mint

Dark rum

Drambuie
Whisky flavored with honey and herbs

Eggs

Frangelico
Hazelnut liqueur

Gin

Ginger beer

Golden rum

Gomme syrup

Grapefruit juice

Green olives

Grenadine
Syrup derived from pomegranates

Ground cinnamon

Ground cloves

Guava juice

Horseradish sauce

Hot pepper sauce

Ice

Irish stout

Kiwi

Lemon juice

Lemons

Lemon vodka
Vodka with a twist of lemon

Light rum

Lime juice

Limes
Mandarin vodka
Vodka with a twist of orange

Mango
Mango juice
Maraschino cherries
Melon liqueur
Milk
Mint leaves
Nutmeg
Orange bitters
Orange Curaçao
Orange juice
Orange liqueur
Oranges
Passion syrup
Peach schnapps
Pepper
Pineapple
Pineapple juice

Ruby Port
Rum-based coffee liqueur
Salt
Soda water
Spiced rum
Sugar cubes
Brown and white

Tequila
Tomato juice
Triple sec
Sweet, white Curaçao

Vermouth
Dry and sweet

Vodka
Whisky/Whiskey
Irish, Scotch and Rye

Worcestershire sauce
Yellow chartreuse
Liqueur flavored with herbs to a secret recipe

FIT FOR DUTY, FIT FOR LIFE

A Training Guide to Accompany Fitness and Lifestyle Management for Law Enforcement

FIFTH EDITION

NANCY WAGNER WISOTZKI

REBECCA FINLAY

emond ▪ Toronto, Canada ▪ 2018

Emond Montgomery Publications Limited
60 Shaftesbury Avenue
Toronto ON M4T 1A3
http://www.emond.ca/highered

Printed in Canada.
Reprinted April 2020.

MIX
Paper from
responsible sources
FSC
www.fsc.org   FSC® C103567

We acknowledge the financial support of the Government of Canada. Canadä

Emond Montgomery Publications has no responsibility for the persistence or accuracy of URLs for external or third-party Internet websites referred to in this publication, and does not guarantee that any content on such websites is, or will remain, accurate or appropriate.

Vice president, publishing: Anthony Rezek
Publisher: Lindsay Sutherland
Director, development and production: Kelly Dickson
Developmental editor: Katherine Goodes
Production supervisor: Laura Bast

Copy editor: Gillian Scobie
Typesetter and text designer: Tara Agnerian
Permissions editor: Lisa Brant
Proofreader: Erin Moore
Cover image: Uber Images/Shutterstock

Library and Archives Canada Cataloguing in Publication

Wagner Wisotzki, Nancy, 1959-, author
    Fit for duty, fit for life : a training guide to accompany Fitness and lifestyle management for law enforcement, fifth edition / Nancy Wagner Wisotzki, Rebecca Finlay.

ISBN 978-1-77255-392-5 (softcover)

    1. Police—Health and hygiene.   2. Police—Physical training.   I. Finlay, Rebecca, author   II. Title.   III. Title: Training guide to accompany Fitness and lifestyle management for law enforcement, fifth edition.   IV. Title: Fitness and lifestyle management for law enforcement.

HV7936.H4W332 2018   613.02'43632   C2018-900413-4

CONTENTS

PREFACE

Fit for Duty, Fit for Life training guide—which accompanies the fifth edition of *Fitness and Lifestyle Management for Law Enforcement*—provides you with the BFOR protocols for various law enforcement agencies and with ideas for training programs that are suitable for your fitness level. The guidebook provides you with the OPFA standards to use as a guide to determine where you are in terms of fitness training. Included at the end of the book are fitness training logs and scoring sheets to track your progress.

ABOUT THE AUTHORS

Nancy Wagner Wisotzki's 35-year career has included being a college professor and coordinator for several programs, including Law and Security, Police Foundations, Bachelor of Human Services (Police Studies), Community and Justice Services, and the Pre-Service Firefighter Education and Training Programs, as well as being a qualified appraiser and trainer for PARE, FITCO, PREP, and COPAT protocols. As a Registered Kinesiologist (HBSc Kin), Certified Exercise Physiologist (CSEP), and EIMC-Recognized Exercise Professional Level 2, her focus is on fitness training and Bona Fide Occupational Requirements (BFOR). She has been a member and on the executive of the Police Fitness Personnel of Ontario for over 25 years. Presently, Nancy is a course conductor for the Ontario Police Fitness Pin Appraisers and continues to work part-time at Georgian College teaching, and conducting BFOR appraisals.

Rebecca Finlay received her Bachelor of Science degree in Kinesiology from the University of Waterloo and is a Certified Exercise Physiologist with the Canadian Society of Exercise Physiology. She currently teaches Fitness and Lifestyle Management at Humber College. She has been involved in police, military, and correctional officer fitness training and testing for over 15 years.

INTRODUCTION

Your commitment to fitness, nutrition, and wellness is paramount to not only your daily life but to the career that you have chosen in law enforcement. The fifth edition of *Fit For Duty, Fit for Life* has been designed to assist you in preparing for the standards set across the province and across Canada.

Bona Fide Occupational Requirements (BFORs) capture the relevant physical duties by job analysis, without over- or under-emphasizing relevant aspects of the job or replicating accurate tasks and complexities of the job. It has been shown that success in the PARE, FITCO, and PREP is related to the training and fitness level of the individual, not height, weight, BMI, or gender (Jamnik, Thomas, Burr, & Gledhill, 2010; Seguin, 2015).

In addition to these components, you will be assessed for health-related matters to determine whether you have the physical capacity for law enforcement work. Without a strong level of fitness, you will not easily achieve the BFOR standards that are set for the program. It is up to you to meet these standards to successfully complete the program. For example, cardiovascular training will assist you in maintaining a positive pace throughout the laps of a circuit, while you navigate stairs and barriers of different heights.

> “ It is the challenge of health and fitness that keeps us striving to stay fit. Embrace the opportunity to push yourself within safe limits that keep you physically, nutritionally, emotionally, and intellectually challenged by your dreams and choices throughout your life. Stay fit and be safe. ”
>
> —Nancy Wisotzki

BONA FIDE OCCUPATIONAL REQUIREMENTS (BFORs)

The following BFORs are used by various law enforcement agencies in Canada. Refer to the Appendix for detailed information on each of the BFORs. Prior to participating in these tests, all participants must be successfully screened with a PAR-Q+—blood pressure and heart rate and signed informed consent form.

PHYSICAL READINESS EVALUATION FOR POLICING (PREP)

The Physical Readiness Evaluation for Policing (PREP) is an occupational assessment that effectively identifies those individuals who possess the physical capabilities needed to meet the rigorous demands of policing.

There are two components to the PREP: a pursuit/restraint circuit that mimics tasks that may be performed on the job and an aerobic shuttle run that tests overall fitness.

The requirements to be successful are:

Pursuit/Restraint Circuit = 157 seconds or less
20-m Shuttle Run = Stage 7

WWW

To watch the PREP instruction video, go to:
https://www.youtube.com/watch?v=zWBPodHpieQ

For additional information on training for PREP go to:
https://www.applicanttesting.com/images/stories/pdf/FittoServe2015Final.pdf

NOTES:

FIGURE 1 PREP Pursuit/Restraint Circuit

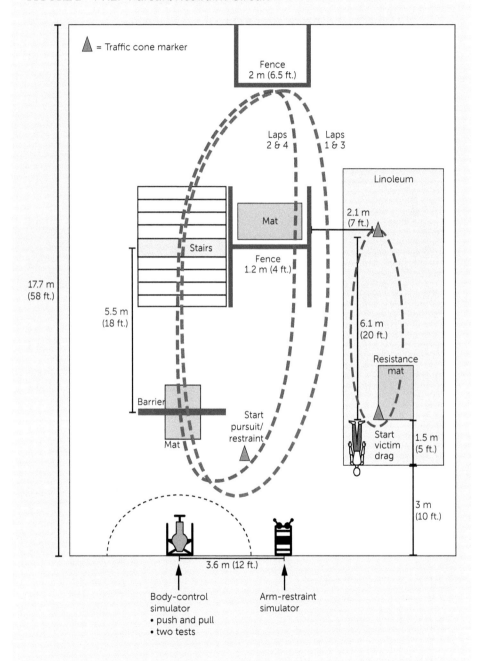

FITNESS TEST FOR CORRECTIONAL OFFICERS (FITCO) IN ONTARIO

In Ontario, the provincial correctional services test their applicants with the Fitness Test for Correctional Officers (FITCO).

There are three performance components to assess your physical capability for the FITCO: Search Station, Emergency Response Circuit, and the 20-m Shuttle Run.

The requirements to be successful are:

Search Station = 120 seconds or less

Emergency Response Circuit = 128 seconds or less

20-m Shuttle Run = Stage 5.5

WWW

To watch the FITCO instruction video, go to:
http://www.mcscs.jus.gov.on.ca/english/corr_serv/careers_in_corr/become _corr_off/FITCO/cs_FITCO.html

For additional information on training for FITCO go to:
http://www.mcscs.jus.gov.on.ca/english/corr_serv/careers_in_corr/become _corr_off/FITCO/cs_FITCO.html

FIGURE 2 FITCO Performance Components

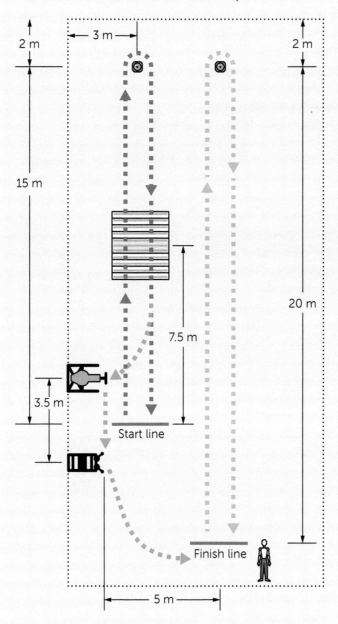

ALBERTA PHYSICAL READINESS EVALUATION FOR POLICING (A-PREP)

The Alberta Physical Readiness Evaluation for Policing was designed to address the specific requirements that police officers face in the province of Alberta.

There are two components to the A-PREP: a pursuit/restraint circuit that mimics tasks that may be performed on the job and an aerobic shuttle run that tests overall fitness.

The requirements to be successful are:

> Pursuit/Restraint Circuit = 130 seconds or less
>
> 20-m Shuttle Run = Stage 7

WWW

To watch the A-PREP instruction video go to:
https://www.youtube.com/watch?v=XJXyVZFVTaA

For additional training information for the A-PREP go to:
http://www.joineps.ca/~/media/Join%20EPS/Files/Alberta%20%20%20Fit%20to%20Serve.ashx

NOTES:

_____

_____

_____

_____

_____

_____

_____

FIGURE 3 A-PREP BFOR

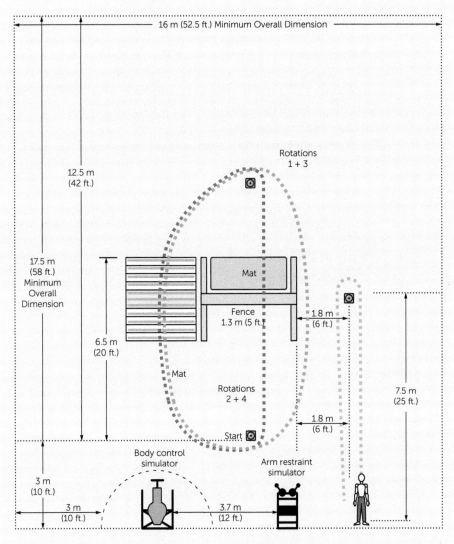

PHYSICAL ABILITIES REQUIREMENT EVALUATION (PARE)

The RCMP Physical Abilities Requirement Evaluation (PARE) is an occupational test used to assess a person's ability to perform the physical demands of police work. It is presently used by Canadian Border Services as a pre-hire requirement and a RCMP cadet exit training requirement. Based on a task analysis of the physical components of police work, the test was designed with three components: the Obstacle Course, the Push/Pull Station, and the Torso Bag Carry.

The requirements to be successful at the conclusion of the RCMP Cadet Training Program are:

> Obstacle Course and Push/Pull Station = 4 minutes or less
>
> Torso Bag Carry (100 lbs.) = completed successfully, no time limit

The requirements to be successful in the Canadian Border Security Officer's application test are:

> Obstacle Course and Push/Pull Station = 4:45 minutes or less
>
> Torso Bag Carry (80 lbs.) = completed successfully, no time limit

WWW

To watch the PARE instructional video go to:
http://www.rcmp-grc.gc.ca/en/pare-demonstration

For additional training information for the PARE go to:
http://www.cbsa-asfc.gc.ca/job-emploi/bso-asf/pare-tape-eng.html#a4

A Comprehensive Functional Strength and Conditioning Program can be found on:

Google Play:
https://play.google.com/store/books/details/luc_poirier_functional_strength _conditioning_progr?id=vmjubaaaqbaj

and iBookstore:
https://itunes.apple.com/ca/book/functional-strength-conditioning/ id891784307?mt=11

FIGURE 4 PARE BFOR

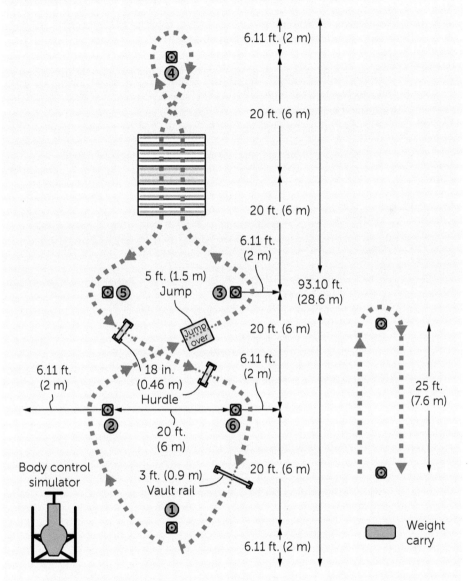

POLICE OFFICER'S PHYSICAL ABILITIES TEST (POPAT)

The POPAT simulates and measures an officer's physical ability to respond to critical incidents, apprehend suspects, and potentially control prisoners.

There are four stations in the POPAT: 440 yard mobility/agility run; pull and push station; modified squat thrust and stand using rail vault; and torso bag carry.

The requirements to be successful are:

The first three stations = 4:45 minutes or less

Torso Bag Carry = completed successfully, no time limit

To watch the POPAT instructional video go to:
https://www.youtube.com/watch?v=vABmYYQvRlA

For the POPAT Male Video:
https://www.youtube.com/watch?v=XSsuLWy6j_Q&t=13s

For the POPAT Female Video:
https://www.youtube.com/watch?v=Tt2QGeRAegM&t=2s_

For additional training information for the POPAT go to:
http://www.saskpolicecollege.ca/fitness/

and:
http://www.lepat.com/fit-popat

NOTES:

FIGURE 5 POPAT BFOR

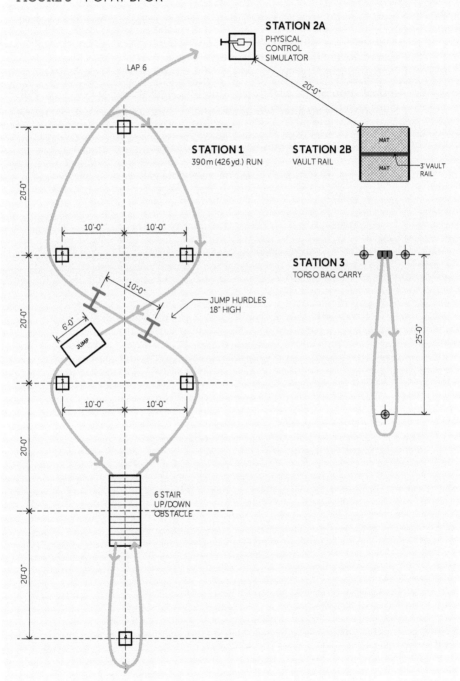

CORRECTIONAL OFFICER'S PHYSICAL ABILITIES TEST (COPAT)

Designed originally as the Canada Federal Correction test, the COPAT has been redesigned and used by various provinces across Canada for a Correctional Officer's BFOR test.

The COPAT has seven stations that need to be completed to be successful: Run 50 m; Stair run; Mobility, Agility, and Speed Run; Pull Station; Push Station; Modified Squat Thrust and Stand; and Weight Carry.

The requirements to be successful are:

> First six stations = 3:20 minutes or less
>
> Weight Carry = completed successfully, no time limit

WWW

To watch the Alberta Public Security COPAT instructional video go to:
https://www.youtube.com/watch?v=rAHzeVetuy8

To watch the Nova Scotia Department of Justice COPAT instructional video go to:
https://www.youtube.com/watch?v=GwdZOyD0GQQ

For additional training information on the COPAT protocol go to:
https://www.solgps.alberta.ca/careers/Publications/COPAT %20Requirements.pdf

FIGURE 6 COPAT BFOR

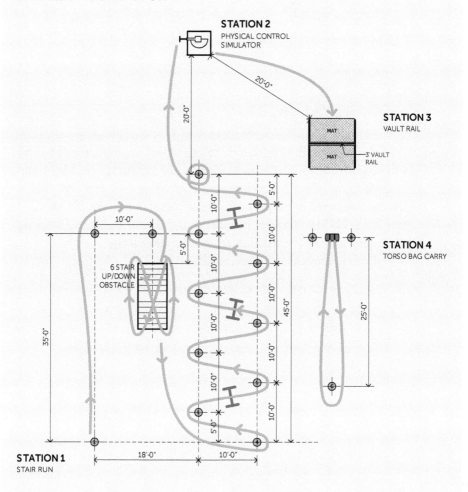

STATION 2
PHYSICAL CONTROL
SIMULATOR

20'-0"

20'-0"

STATION 3
VAULT RAIL

MAT

MAT

3' VAULT
RAIL

10'-0"

5'-0"

10'-0"

STATION 4
TORSO BAG CARRY

10'-0"

5'-0"

6 STAIR
UP/DOWN
OBSTACLE

10'-0"

10'-0"

10'-0"

45'-0"

25'-0"

35'-0"

10'-0"

10'-0"

5'-0"

STATION 1
STAIR RUN

18'-0"

10'-0"

SPAT-ENPQ

Quebec has redesigned the Standardized Physical Abilities Test–École nationale de Police du Québec (SPAT-ENPQ 2017). For more information regarding the test and training, go to http://www.enpq.qc.ca/futur -policier/esap-enpq.html for the updates in French. Updates in English are to follow.

FORCE EVALUATION

The FORCE Evaluation is a measure of operational fitness, designed by the Canadian Armed Forces (CAF) to reflect the minimum physical standard required for duties of service. The FORCE Evaluation is designed to capture the movement patterns, energy systems, and muscle groups recruited in the performance of common military duties.

The FORCE Evaluation includes four tasks: 20-m Rushes, Sandbag Lift, Intermittent Loaded Shuttles, and Sandbag Drag.

The requirements to be successful are:

> 20-m Rushes = 51 seconds or less
> Sandbag Lift = 30 repetitions in 3:30 minutes or less
> Intermittent Loaded Shuttles = 5:21 minutes or less
> Sandbag Drag = complete 20-m drag without stopping

NOTES:

FORCE EVALUATION COMPONENTS

FIGURE 7 20-Metre Rushes Floor Plan

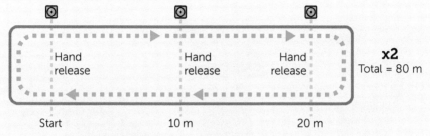

SOURCE: Canadian Forces Morale and Welfare Services, 2016, p. 38.

FIGURE 8 Sandbag Lift Wall Plan

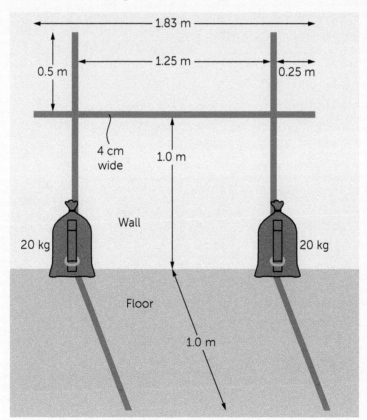

SOURCE: Canadian Forces Morale and Welfare Services, 2016, p. 16.

FIGURE 9   Acceptable Sandbag Safe Techniques

SOURCE: Canadian Forces Morale and Welfare Services, 2016, p. 43.

FIGURE 10   Intermittent Loaded Shuttles Floor Plan

SOURCE: Canadian Forces Morale and Welfare Services, 2016, p. 17.

FIGURE 11 Sandbag Drag Floor Plan

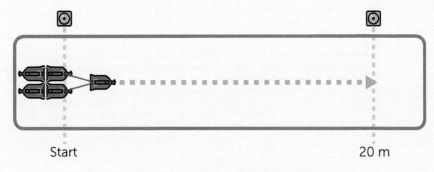

Start   20 m

SOURCE: Canadian Forces Morale and Welfare Services, 2016, p. 19.

To watch the FORCE Evaluation instructional video, go to:
https://www.cfmws.com/en/AboutUs/PSP/DFIT/Fitness/FORCEprogram/
Pages/FORCE_videos.aspx

For additional training for the FORCE Evaluation go to:
https://www.cfmws.com/en/AboutUs/PSP/DFIT/Fitness/FORCEprogram/
Documents/FORCE%20Operation%20Manual%20PDFs/FORCE%20Operation
%20Manual.pdf

GETTING STARTED

BASIC RECOMMENDATIONS FOR PHYSICAL ACTIVITY GUIDELINES

Both the Canadian Society of Exercise Physiology (CSEP, 2011) and the American College of Sports Medicine (Garber et al., 2011) have released recommended quantity and quality guidelines for an exercise prescription for adults. The following chart will provide you with the guidelines for creating your own program.

TABLE 1 Physical Activity Guidelines

TYPE OF EXERCISE	QUANTITY AND QUALITY OF ACTIVITY
Cardio-respiratory Exercise	• participate in at least 150 minutes of moderate-intensity exercise per week (i.e., 30–60 minutes of moderate-intensity five days a week). • one continuous session or multiple shorter sessions (at least 10 minutes) are acceptable to accumulate desired amount of daily exercise. • gradual progression of exercise time, frequency, and intensity is recommended for best adherence and least injury risk. • if you are unable to meet the minimum, you can still benefit from some activity. • more physical activity provides greater health benefits. • more intense activity results in performance gains.
Resistance Exercise	• train each major muscle group at least two or three days each week using a variety of exercises and equipment. • very light or light intensity is best for previously sedentary adults starting exercise. • two to four sets of each exercise will help adults improve strength and power. • it is important to allow muscle groups to rest for 48 hours between resistance training sessions.

TYPE OF EXERCISE	QUANTITY AND QUALITY OF ACTIVITY
Flexibility Exercise	• perform flexibility exercises every day to improve range of motion. • muscles should feel tight when stretched, but not in pain. • stretches should be held for 20–30 seconds, or until muscle tightness starts to ease. • repeat each stretch two to four times, accumulating 60 seconds per stretch. • static, dynamic, and PNF stretches are all effective. • performing flexibility exercises are most effective when the muscle is warm—perform an active warm up or do your flexibility exercises at the end of your workout.
Neuromotor Exercise	• neuromotor exercises are recommended at least two or three days per week. • exercises should involve motor skills (balance, agility, coordination, and gait), proprioceptive exercise training, and multifaceted activities (tai chi and yoga) to improve physical function and prevent falls in older adults. • 20–30 minutes is appropriate for neuromotor exercises.

SOURCES: CSEP, 2011; Garber et al., 2011.

IMPORTANCE OF AN ACTIVE WARM-UP

An active warm-up is an essential component of an exercise program. The intent of a warm-up is to increase the body temperature, heart rate, and blood flow and to prepare the body for the demands of the conditioning phase. The length of a warm-up depends on several factors, including the type of activity, intensity level, and the participant's age and fitness level. According to the ACSM guidelines (Thompson, et al., 2010) an aerobic activity warm-up should consist of a minimum of five to ten minutes of low- to moderate-level activity.

A warm-up should include light aerobic endurance activities (e.g., jumping jacks, skipping, and light jogging) coupled with dynamic stretches that mimic movements of the activity you are doing. Dynamic stretching is when a muscle group is taken through a controlled movement to improve range of motion and loosen up the muscles while mimicking the type of workout that you are going to do. If you are going to be challenging yourself to a timed 1.5-mile run then doing some high knees, heel kicks, and leg sweeps would be suitable. If you are going to do an upper body workout it would be appropriate to do shoulder rolls, arm circles, and arm swings.

A warm-up may produce mild sweating but should not leave you fatigued. To avoid an accident (i.e., tearing of muscles) you need to make sure that the warm-up is appropriate for the intensity and length of the workout. So, the higher the intensity, the longer the warm-up should be (Bushman, 2017).

EXAMPLES OF DYNAMIC STRETCHING EXERCISES

The following dynamic stretches will help prepare you for your workout as well as any of the BFOR tests. As you do the stretches, start with slow controlled movements and then increase the speed as you increase your range of motion and improve your kinesthetic awareness, or "muscle memory."

SHOULDER ROLLS

Stand with your feet shoulder-width apart and your spine neutral. Roll your shoulders up and back smoothly and under control, going through a full range of motion. Continue motion for approximately 10 to 15 seconds and then switch directions.

FIGURE 12   Shoulder Rolls

ARM CIRCLES

Stand with your feet shoulder-width apart and your spine neutral. With your arms out to the side, start making small circles with your hands and build up to large circles. Circles should be smooth and under control, going through a full range of motion of the shoulder. Continue motion for approximately 10 to 15 seconds and then switch directions.

FIGURE 13 Arm Circles

NOTES:

ARM SWINGS

Stand with your feet shoulder-width apart and your spine neutral, swing your arms back and forth in front of your body. Swings can start out small, but increase so that you allow them to swing to full range of motion in the front and back. Continue motion for approximately 10 to 15 seconds.

FIGURE 14 Arm Swings

NOTES:

HIP ROTATIONS

With your hands on your hips and feet slightly wider than shoulder-width apart, move your hips in a big circular motion. Continue for 10 to 15 seconds and then switch directions.

FIGURE 15 Hip Rotations

HEEL KICKS

Stand with your feet slightly wider than shoulder-width apart and kick one heel up behind you. Then switch and allow your other heel to kick up behind you. It should feel like walking with exaggerated backswings of your heels. Continue motion for approximately 10 to 15 seconds. This can also be done while walking or jogging.

FIGURE 16 Heel Kicks

HIGH KNEES

Stand with your feet close together and bring one knee up in front of you. Then switch and bring the other knee up in front. It should feel like walking with exaggerated high knees. Continue motion for approximately 10 to 15 seconds. This can also be done while walking, skipping, or jogging.

FIGURE 17   High Knees

LEG SWINGS

Stand on your right foot, placing your left hand on the wall for balance, and keep your torso in an upright position. Swing your left leg forward and backward, trying to go through the full range of motion of your hips. Continue motion for 10 to 15 seconds and then switch legs.

FIGURE 18   Forward Leg Swings

You can also face the wall and do leg sweeps laterally, allowing your leg to swing side to side.

FIGURE 19   Lateral Leg Swings

LATERAL SIDE MOVEMENTS

Stand with feet shoulder-width apart and keeping your knees bent, take a big step to the left side, with your left foot and then step your right foot to the left. Keep moving sideways for four or five big steps and then switch directions, leading with the other foot. This can also be done by leaping or hopping your steps side to side.

FIGURE 20   Lateral Side Movements

NOTES:

FORWARD LUNGES

Stand tall, with your shoulders back, chest up, and eyes looking straight ahead. Take a big step forwards with one leg, bending your front knee and lower down until your thigh is parallel to the ground. Your back knee should come down to within an inch of the ground, allowing your back heel to come off the ground. Push off your front foot, and return up to a standing position. Do approximately five repetitions and then switch legs.

FIGURE 21 Forward Lunges

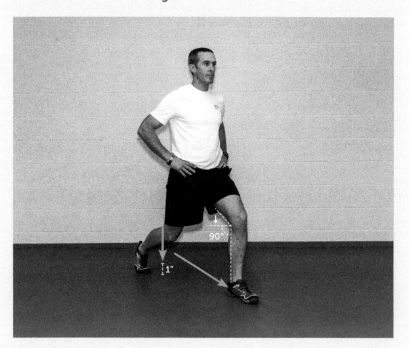

SIDE LUNGES

Stand with your feet very wide, and leaning forward slightly at the hips, shift your body side to side from one foot to the other foot, keeping your knee over the foot of your bent leg. Allow a few seconds to pause with your body over one foot to stretch your adductors.

FIGURE 22   Side Lunges

NOTES:

TRAINING WORKOUTS

Preparing for a career in Canadian law enforcement and its mandatory BFOR requires you to be participating in a resistance training program. Every BFOR has components that necessitate strength, endurance, agility, and coordination. To be properly preparing, you should be training at least three times a week. Depending on your fitness level, the amount of time you have to train, and the equipment you have available to you, there are a number of different types of workouts that you could do. Chapter 6 of *Fitness and Lifestyle Management for Law Enforcement* outlines how to design your individual resistance training program, with explanations on how to arrange exercises, decide on sets/reps, and choose your appropriate weight. In Chapter 6 you can also learn the difference between different types of training methods, including circuit training, light to heavy, heavy to light, pyramid, superset, triset, and functional training.

GUIDELINES FOR RESISTANCE TRAINING

Here is a reminder of the guidelines of resistance training in respect to your goals. When training for a BFOR it is important that you are incorporating all principles of resistance training into your program, as most BFORs include aspects of each. And to complement your resistance training program, make sure that you are also including cardiovascular training as well.

TABLE 2   Guidelines for Resistance Training

TRAINING GOAL	# OF REPS	# OF SETS	REST BETWEEN SETS
Muscular Endurance	12–25	1–3	30–60 seconds
Hypertrophy	6–12	3–6	30–90 seconds
Strength	1–6	3–6	2–5 minutes
Power	1–5	3–5	2–5 minutes

SOURCES: CSEP, 2011; Garber et al., 2011.

The *Fit for Duty, Fit for Life* training guide was designed specifically to prepare you for task-specific law enforcement requirements. There are eight specific movement domains that need to be practised and mastered to complete most BFOR tests:

1. Push exercises
2. Pull exercises
3. Arm restraint exercises
4. Grip strength exercises
5. Heavy object relocation exercises
6. Agility training
7. Running training
8. Core training

The *Fit for Duty, Fit for Life* training guide will provide you with many different exercises for each of the components. Most exercises offer variations of equipment and position, as well as beginner and advanced modifications. Pick and choose exercises based on your goals, what you need to improve on, and the BFOR you are training for.

Try to balance your workouts: push exercises with pull exercises, resistance training with cardiovascular training, and strength exercises with endurance exercises. To evaluate your progress, we suggest that you make use of the resistance training and running logs at the end of this guide to assist you in monitoring your results so that you have the ability to modify if required and reward your achievements.

NOTES:

FYI

TIPS FOR RESISTANCE TRAINING

Effective resistance training depends on proper technique and execution. Follow these basic rules to maximize your weight training program.

- Ensure that you have the correct technique. In this guide we have described and displayed pictures of each exercise, but it is vital that you are doing the exercise correctly. Ask a fitness specialist to watch your technique and correct your form.
- Choose the proper weight. If the weight is too much, you may have trouble lifting it and start recruiting other muscles to help, instead of isolating the correct muscle. It is better to start out with a lighter weight and work your way up.
- Control the weight. Make sure that you are lifting the weight under control and that you are not lifting too fast or bouncing the weight. Not only do you want to control the weight through the concentric contraction, but also through the eccentric contraction.
- Maintain a neutral spinal position. In its neutral position, your spine has three curves between your head and your pelvis. Your neck and low back have inward curves (lordosis) and your mid-back curves outward (kyphosis). Maintaining these three curves (a neutral spine) is critical when lifting weights as it helps distribute your weight linearly through your vertebral column. This allows your vertebral discs to cushion the impact of the exercise and is vital in limiting your risk of a back injury.

PUSH EXERCISES

Push exercises are necessary to successfully manipulate the Body Control Simulator, which is used in the PREP, FITCO, A-PREP, PARE, POPAT, COPAT, and SPAT-ENPQ BFORs.

The Body Control Simulator (also known as the Push/Pull machine) simulates an altercation with an individual at an "emergency pace" in a controlled manner. The push phase involves pushing the handles away from you and lifting the weights (which requires forces of 31.5/35.5/38.6 kg depending on protocol) off the cradle and moving left or right depending on the instructions given. It is important for you to push straight along the main rod, so placing your hands at hip height is key. Throughout the push, your arms must be slightly bent at all times and your chest must not be touching either the handles or your hands. While moving from side to side, you must not allow the weights to touch the base.

FIGURE 23 Push Component on the Body Control Simulator

The following exercises have been suggested to help prepare you for all of the push components of the tests. Pushing requires training the chest, shoulders, triceps, legs, and core.

CHEST PRESS

Lie flat on a bench, stability ball, or other surface with your feet flat on the floor or the bench. Start with the dumbbells at chest height and then press them upward until your arms are fully straight, with a neutral grip. Lower the dumbbells until they are level with your chest.

FIGURE 24   Chest Press

Variations include:
- use a barbell and weights
- use a chest press machine
- use different grips and hand placements
- adjust the angle on the bench (incline or decline)

PUSH-UP

Lie flat on your stomach, legs together, hands positioned under the shoulders, fingers facing forward. Push up from the floor by fully straightening the elbows, using the toes as the pivotal point (for modified push-ups pivot from the knees). The body must be kept in a straight line. Then lower yourself until your chin touches the floor.

FIGURE 25 Push-Up

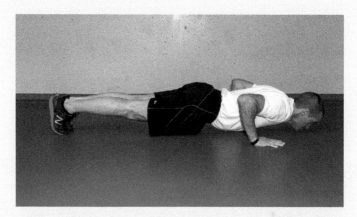

Variations include:

- place hands on a bench or higher surface
- place one hand on a medicine ball or dumbbell
- place feet on a stability ball or a bench
- different hand positions (wide and narrow)

SLED PUSH

Load the sled or prowler with your desired weight. Stand behind the sled and place your hands on the handles/bar. Lean into the sled, fully extending your arms. Push the sled as far and as fast as possible, by driving with the legs.

FIGURE 26   Sled Push

SHOULDER PRESS

Sitting upright on a bench, stability ball, or chair, grasp a dumbbell in each hand and hold them at shoulder height. With hands facing forward, press the dumbbells up over your head until arms are fully straight. Lower the dumbbells until they are level with your shoulders.

FIGURE 27   Shoulder Press

Variations include:

- adjust the angle on the bench to incline
- use a barbell and weights
- use a shoulder press machine
- use a Smith machine
- use a resistance band fixed under your feet
- do exercise from a standing position
- include a squat with the shoulder press

HANDSTAND

Facing a wall, place your hands on the floor 5 to 8 inches (13 to 20 cm) away from the wall. Kick your legs up, fully extended until your feet hit the wall under control. Keep your hips close to the wall and body straight. Practise bringing one foot away from the wall and then both, until you can balance without the wall.

FIGURE 28   Handstand

Variations include:
- handstand pushups—bending at the elbow and lowering your body toward the floor
- free-standing handstand
- free-standing handstand with legs out to the side

LATERAL RAISE

From a standing position, feet shoulder-width apart, hold dumbbells at the side of your body. Lift dumbbells out to the side, to shoulder height. Lower them down under control.

FIGURE 29 Lateral Raise

Variations include:

- use a resistance band fixed under your feet
- use cables

NOTES:

FRONT RAISE

From a standing position, feet shoulder-width apart, hold dumbbells in front of your body. Lift dumbbells up to the front, up to shoulder height. Lower them down under control.

FIGURE 30 Front Raise

Variations include:
- use a resistance band fixed under your feet
- use cables
- use a barbell
- use a weight plate

NOTES:

BENCH DIP

Sitting on the edge of a bench, grasp the edge of the bench with your hands right beside your hips. With your legs straight out in front of you, bring your hips forward slightly so that you just clear the bench while maintaining your hand grip on the bench. Lower your body toward the floor by bending your arms, while keeping a neutral spine. Then straighten your arms to full extension.

FIGURE 31 Bench Dip

Variations include:
- place feet under knees (beginner position)
- place your feet up on another bench or higher surface (advanced position)
- use a triceps dip machine
- use parallel dip bars

OVERHEAD TRICEPS EXTENSION

Attach a bar, handle, or rope to the cable and choose your desired weight. Grasp the bar behind your head and turn to face away from the pulley. With one foot in front of the other, bend slightly at the knees to help with balance. Your upper arms should be close to parallel with the floor, with your elbows bent and hands facing up. Push the bar out in front of your body until your arms are fully extended. Bend your elbows to return it to the start position.

FIGURE 32 Overhead Triceps Extension

Variations include:
- triceps extensions (arms straight over head, lower dumbbell by bending elbow)
- from seated, lying, standing positions
- use dumbbells, barbells, kettlebells
- single arm or both arms

SQUAT

Stand with your feet a little bit wider than shoulder-width apart. Brace your core and bend at your knees and hips, like you are sitting down on an imaginary stool. Squat down as low as you can while maintaining a neutral spine. Press up through your heels and squeeze your glutes, as you stand back up to straight.

FIGURE 33   Squat

Variations include:
- hold a barbell on the back of your neck/shoulders
- use a Smith machine
- hold dumbbells at your shoulders, or by your sides

WALL SIT

With your back flat against a wall, place your feet about 50 cm away from the wall, shoulder-width apart. Slide your back down the wall, so that your thighs are parallel with the ground, your knees bent at a 90-degree angle and your knees over your feet. Hands should not be resting on legs.

FIGURE 34   Wall Sit

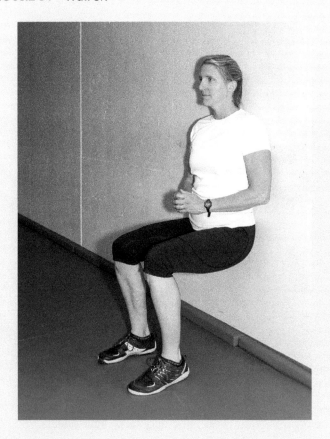

Variations include:
- change position of feet (feet together, feet wide apart)
- hold a weight in your hands
- single leg hold

LEG PRESS

Choose desired weight for machine. Place your feet on the platform, slightly wider than shoulder-width. Depending on the type of machine, you will either start from a bent knee position or a straight leg position (shown in picture). Lower the platform by bending your legs as low as you can while maintaining a neutral spine. Push the platform back up until your legs are straight.

FIGURE 35 Leg Press

LUNGES

Stand tall, with your shoulders back, chest up, and eyes looking straight ahead. Take a big step forwards with one leg, bending your front leg and lowering down until your thigh is parallel to the ground, your knee over your foot. Your back knee should come down to within a few centimetres of the ground, allowing your back heel to come up off the ground. Push off your front foot, and squeeze your glutes to return up to a standing position.

FIGURE 36 Lunges

Variations include:
- reverse lunges (step backwards)
- alternate legs
- walking lunges—with each lunge continue to step forward as you alternate
- hold dumbbells at shoulders or sides
- hold a barbell on the back of your neck/shoulders

FOREARM PLANK

Place forearms on the ground with the elbows aligned below the shoulders and hands together or palms flat on floor. Plant your toes on the floor and press up through your hip, so that your body is a straight line from your head to your ankles. Focus on activating core muscles. Hold for desired length of time.

FIGURE 37   Forearm Plank

Variations include:
- plank from knees (beginner position)
- plank from hands, arms straight
- move from forearms to hands and back
- lift one leg
- rotate to a side bridge

PULL EXERCISES

Pull exercises are used to help you train for the Body Control Simulator (PREP, FITCO, A-PREP, PARE, POPAT, COPAT, and SPAT-ENPQ), the Sandbag Drag (FORCE evaluation), and Victim Relocation (PREP, FITCO, A-PREP, and SPAT-ENPQ).

The pull component of the Body Control Simulator involves pulling the handle or rope toward you to lift the weight (which requires forces of 31.5/35.5/38.6 kg depending on protocol) off the cradle and while holding the weight up, either using the method of shuffle stepping or crossing feet, you will move to the left or right depending on the protocol instructions. It is imperative that you learn to pull and squat down so that your thighs are parallel to the floor and your elbows bent. While moving from side to side, you must not allow the weights to touch the base.

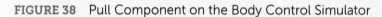

FIGURE 38 Pull Component on the Body Control Simulator

The following exercises have been suggested to help prepare you for all of the pull components of the tests. Pulling requires training the back, biceps, legs, and core.

LAT PULL DOWN

Choose your desired weight on the machine and adjust the pad so that when you sit down it is right on top of your legs. Grasp the bar with a wide overhand grip. Sit down with your arms fully extended. Pull the bar down to your chest, keeping your chin back, spine neutral, and chest lifted. Straighten your arms back to the start position.

FIGURE 39   Lat Pull Down

Variations include:
- use a resistance band attached to a fixed point
- pull-ups
- assisted pull-up machine

CABLE ROW

Choose your desired weight and adjust the cable so that it is approximately waist height. With both hands on a two-handed row attachment, sit back (with a neutral spine) and lift the weight with your arms extended. Pull the handle to your stomach and squeeze your shoulder blades back and together. In this position you can practise moving side to side to simulate the movement required for the Body Control Simulator or keep your feet planted and straighten your arms for another repetition.

FIGURE 40   Cable Row

SEATED ROW

Choose your desired weight and sit down with your back straight. Pick up the two-handed row attachment with straight arms and slide back until your legs are almost fully extended with just a slight bend in your knees. Pull the handle to your stomach and squeeze your shoulder blades back and together. Straighten your arms back out under control, while maintaining a neutral spine.

FIGURE 41   Seated Row

Variations include:
- use a resistance band attached to a fixed point

BENT OVER ROW

Holding dumbbells, bend forward at your waist, keeping a neutral spine. Allow your arms to fully extend down with your hands in a neutral position. Pull the dumbbells up to your hips, squeezing your shoulder blades back and together.

FIGURE 42   Bent Over Row

Variations include:
- use a barbell
- one arm row with opposite knee and hand on a bench or other surface

SLED DRAG

Grasping a rope attached to a loaded sled, prowler, or a sandbag, sit back with your arms slightly bent and your spine neutral. Pull object moving backwards and, if possible, moving side to side as well.

FIGURE 43   Sled Drag

NOTES:

BATTLING ROPES EXERCISES

Stand with feet wide and knees bent in an athletic stance. Hold the ends of the ropes at arm's length, hands shoulder-width apart. Brace your core and begin alternately raising and lowering your arms explosively, to create waves in the ropes.

FIGURE 44   Battle Ropes

Variations include:
- move ropes in circles
- move ropes side to side
- cross overs—hands together, arc your arms over your head and slam the ropes into the ground

CHIN UP

Grasp the chin-up bar with an underhand grip, hands approximately 15 to 20 cm apart. Pull yourself up so that your chin is over the bar. Lower yourself until your arms are fully extended.

FIGURE 45   Chin Up

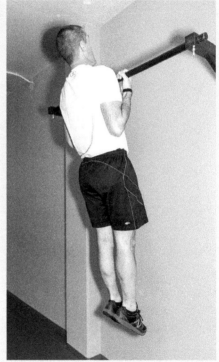

Variations include:
- use an assisted chin-up machine
- use different grips and hand placements

BICEP CURL

Standing straight, hold dumbbells at your sides. Curl the dumbbells up to your shoulders, keeping elbows by your sides. Lower the dumbbells back down until arms are straight. Palms can be facing forwards/open, at a 45-degree angle, or inwards for a hammer curl.

FIGURE 46 Bicep Curl

Variations include:
- use a barbell
- use a resistance band fixed under your feet
- use cable
- from sitting position
- single arm, concentration curl

CORE ENDURANCE ASSESSMENT

The PFPO are using the modified Sorrenson Test as their core endurance assessment. Refer to the Core Endurance Assessment below in OPFA standards.

FIGURE 47 Core Endurance

NOTES:

ARM RESTRAINT EXERCISES

Used in the PREP, A-PREP and FITCO, the Arm Retraction Simulator simulates forces to grip (14.5 to 26 kg) and retract (16 or 28.5 kg depending on protocol) the arms of a noncompliant individual, similar to the movements required to place an individual in handcuffs.

In the PREP and A-PREP protocols, you are required to grasp both handles with your fingers and thumbs wrapped around the grip and fully depress the handles and then bring them together until the two collars touch.

FIGURE 48 PREP Arm Restraint

In the FITCO protocol you position your feet so that the handle is midline to the body. You then grasp the one handle with your two hands and squeeze the lever until it is fully depressed. Without moving your feet and maintaining adequate grip strength to keep the lever depressed through the movement, bring the handle toward the middle of the machine so that it passes the indicator line and then return it to the starting position in a controlled manner. Move to the other handle and repeat the process.

The following exercises have been suggested to help prepare you for the arm restraint component of the test. Exercises focus on training the chest.

PEC DECK FLY

Choose your desired weight. Depending on the type of machine, there will either be handles to grasp (shown in picture) or pads for your arms to be bent. Bring the handles (or pads) together, squeezing your chest. Return handles (or pads) to start position, ideally so that your chest is open wide.

FIGURE 49   Pec Deck Fly

CHEST FLY

Lie on a bench, stability ball, or other surface and hold the dumbbells together with palms facing each other. Straighten your arms up above your chest, with a slight bend at the elbow. Lower the dumbbells down to the sides of your chest, in a large semicircular motion. Return your arms back up to the top following the same curve.

FIGURE 50   Chest Fly

Variations include:
- change the position of the bench (incline or decline)
- use cables

CABLE CHEST PRESS

Choose your desired weight and adjust cables to shoulder height. Step forward with one foot and with hands at sides of chest pull weights up. Press hands forward and together with arms as straight as possible. Lower weights under control, bringing hands back to side of chest.

FIGURE 51   Cable Chest Press

Variations include:
  • cable crossover

GRIP STRENGTH EXERCISES

Grip strength is an important component in all the BFOR protocols. Each BFOR requires you to have adequate grip strength to complete certain tasks. These tasks include the Arm Restraint (PREP, FITCO, A-PREP, and SPAT-ENPQ), Mattress Hold (FITCO), Torso Bag Carry (PARE, POPAT, and COPAT), Sandbag Lift/Carry (FORCE Evaluation), and Relocating Over Barriers (PREP, A-PREP, PARE, and SPAT-ENPQ).

Handgrip strength is a measurement of isometric strength. Controlling a non-compliant individual, handcuffing an individual, grappling for a weapon, or holding and aiming a firearm all require hand strength and wrist control.

FIGURE 52 Different Grips Required

a) Torso Bag Carry

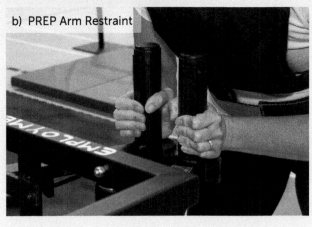

b) PREP Arm Restraint

FYI

TIPS REGARDING GRIP STRENGTH

FIGURE 53   Dumbbell Training

- Grip strength will increase if you are using dumbbells when training, as opposed to machines. Wrapping your hand tightly around a dumbbell uses more forearm strength than when you are using a machine for your exercises.

FIGURE 54   Fat Grip Holds

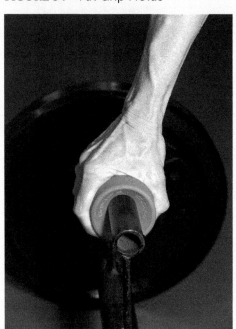

- Making a grip fatter requires more grip strength than holding a regular bar or dumbbell. Whenever possible make your grip wider by adding Fat Grip Holds, or wrapping a towel around the bar or dumbbell. Gripping the top of a Hex dumbbell is also a great way to make the grip more challenging.

The following exercises have been suggested to help prepare you for the grip strength components of the tests. These exercises focus on training the forearms and upper body.

GRIP SQUEEZE

Using grip-squeezing handles or ball, squeeze hand tightly around it and then relax grip.

FIGURE 55   Grip Squeeze

NOTES:

_____

_____

_____

_____

_____

FARMER'S WALK

Grasp farmer's walk handles by your sides and lift them by driving through your heels, keep your back straight and head up. Walk the desired distance. Arms hang by your sides, keep core muscles activated, spine neutral, and eyes looking straight ahead.

FIGURE 56 Farmer's Walk

Variations include:

- use kettlebells
- use dumbbells
- pinch weight plates

TWO ARM HANG

Grasp a chin-up bar with an overhand grip slightly wider than shoulder-width and hang with feet off of the floor for your desired length of time.

FIGURE 57 Two Arm Hang

Variations include:
- loop two towels over a bar and hang from them
- hang from rope wrapped around bar
- single arm hang

WRIST ROLL

Hold bar straight out in front of you. Rotate one wrist forward, followed by the other until the entire rope is wrapped up around the roller. Then roll wrists the other direction one at a time to let the rope back down again.

FIGURE 58   Wrist Roll

NOTES:

_____

_____

_____

_____

_____

_____

_____

STRAIGHT ARM HOLD

Stand with feet shoulder-width apart, spine neutral, and hold up a weighted object in front of your body. The object should be held away from your body, with your arms as straight as possible. Hold in place for your desired length of time. (To reflect the weight of the mattress used for the FITCO test, use a weight equal or heavier than 12.3 kg.)

FIGURE 59   Straight Arm Hold

Variations include:
- hold a gym mat
- hold a FITCO mattress
- hold a dumbbell
- hold a weight plate
- hold a barbell

HEAVY OBJECT RELOCATION EXERCISES

All of the BFOR protocols require you to relocate either a victim or a heavy bag of various weights to simulate the removal of individuals from scenarios or assist with building a wall with multiple sandbag fills and carries. Examples include 39 to 77 kg Victim Relocation (PREP, FITCO, A-PREP, and SPAT-ENPQ), 36 to 45.4 kg Torso Bag Carry (PARE, POPAT, and COPAT), and 20 kg Sandbag Lift/Carry (FORCE Evaluation). Lifting and carrying heavier objects require proper techniques.

FIGURE 60   Heavy Object Relocation

a) Victim Relocation

b) Torso Bag Carry

The following are exercises designed to help you train to lift, pull, and relocate heavy objects. Exercises focus on training legs and shoulders.

SLED DRAG

Refer to Pull Exercises for explanation and photo.

SQUAT

Refer to Push Exercises for explanation and photo.

DEADLIFT

Stand with your feet shoulder-width apart, flat on the floor and beneath the bar. Keeping your spine neutral, and with a slight bend in your hips and knees, grip the bar so that your hands are just outside of your thighs. With your chin up and eyes facing straight ahead, stand up with the barbell, squeezing your glutes and hamstrings. Make sure you come all the way up to straight so that your chest is up and shoulders are back and your hips, knees, and feet form a straight line. Lower the bar back down, keeping it close to your legs as you bend your legs and maintain a neutral spine.

FIGURE 61 Deadlifts

Variations include:
- use dumbbells
- use kettlebells

CALF RAISE

Stand with your toes up on a ledge (or on the floor). Place your hand on a wall or object for balance and push up as high as you can onto your toes. Lower back down.

FIGURE 62 Calf Raise

Variations include:
- use a calf raises machine
- use a leg press (fully straighten your legs and push up onto your toes)
- hold weights (dumbbells, barbell, weight plate)

LEG EXTENSION

Sit down, choose your desired weight and adjust the machine according to your body. Hook your feet beneath the roller pads and grasp the handles at the sides of the machine. Straighten your legs and lift the weight up. Lower the weight to the starting position.

FIGURE 63 Leg Extension

HAMSTRING CURL

Sit down, choose your desired weight and adjust the machine according to your body. Place the backs of your lower legs on the pads. The lap pad should be against your thighs, just above your knee. Press your feet down, bringing the pad under your seat. Raise the pad back up to the starting position.

FIGURE 64   Hamstring Curl

Variations include:
- use a stability ball (in a push-up position, with your feet on the ball, roll the ball toward your hands, bending your knees)

ONE LEG SPLIT SQUAT

Position yourself in a staggered stance, one foot underneath you and your rear foot elevated on a bench. Lower your body straight down until your back knee gets close to the floor. Stand up by squeezing glutes.

FIGURE 65   One Leg Split Squat

Variations include:
- rear foot on the floor
- rear foot on an unstable surface (Bosu Ball, stability ball)
- hold dumbbells by your side

ABDUCTOR (SIDE LEG LIFT)

Lie on your side, with your bottom leg bent at a 90-degree angle and your thighs parallel with each other. Raise your top leg up as far as you can without twisting through your spine. Keep your foot flexed and your leg straight as you lift. Lower it back down to within a few centimetres of the ground.

FIGURE 66   Side Leg Lift

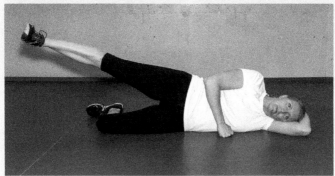

Variations include:
- With your top leg in the air you can do
  - small pulses
  - small circles
  - large circles
  - point and flex your foot
  - flex and extend your knee
- use an abductor machine
- use a resistance band, from a standing or lying position
- use cables

SHOULDER SHRUG

Standing tall with dumbbells in each hand, shrug your shoulders up as high as you can toward your ears. Lower back down to the start position.

FIGURE 67   Shoulder Shrug

Variations include:
- use a barbell
- use kettlebells

UPRIGHT ROW

Standing tall with dumbbells in each hand, and palms facing body, lift the dumbbells up until your hands are just above your chest area. Your elbows should come up just as high as your shoulders. Resist the urge to shrug your shoulders. Lower back down to start position.

FIGURE 68   Upright Row

Variations include:
- use a barbell
- use a resistance band fixed under your feet
- use a cable
- use kettlebells

SUITCASE CARRY

With feet shoulder-width apart, flex your knees and hips into a deadlift position with a neutral spine. Hold a weight in one hand (kettlebell, dumbbell, weight plates), and lift up the weight by extending through the hips and knees. Brace your core and walk desired distance while maintaining a straight spine.

FIGURE 69 Suitcase Carry

FARMER'S WALK

Refer to Grip Strength for explanation and photo.

AGILITY CIRCUIT EXERCISES

Agility is the ability to change directions with your body quickly and efficiently. It is essential in law enforcement job-related tasks. Each BFOR has an agility component (e.g., running stairs, moving around pylons, jumping, crawling while completing pursuit circuits), which makes it crucial to add agility exercises and plyometric drills into your training. Additionally, by adding balance, mobility, and other functional training movements, which reflect the BFOR tasks, it will help you pass these skill-related abilities tests.

Start with one or two days per week. It is important to incorporate a thorough warm-up with dynamic movements that will mimic the agility exercises, to prevent injury and enhance joint and muscle flexibility.

FIGURE 70   Agility Requirements

a) Crawling under Barrier

b) Jumping over Vault

The following are some examples of exercises that will help improve agility, speed, coordination, and power. You can do some of the exercises on the spot with minimal equipment, or you can set up a circuit that will require some space and equipment.

JUMPS

Make sure that when you are jumping, you are landing softly on your toes with a slight bend in your knees. Feel free to use your arms to help propel you as well.

Here are a few variations of jumps:

- Tuck jump—feet shoulder-width apart, bend your knees and powerfully jump straight up bringing your knees toward your chest.

FIGURE 71 Tuck Jump

- Squat jump—feet shoulder-width apart, squat down until your upper thighs are parallel to the ground and then powerfully jump straight up.
- Lateral jump—feet close together, bend your knees and then jump to the side, either focusing on distance or height.

BURPEES

Begin by standing with feet shoulder-width apart. Hop down to a crouch position, hands on the ground, knees tucked under your torso (1st position). Kick your feet out simultaneously to a plank position, keeping your arms extended under your chest (2nd position). Return your feet back under to the crouch position (3rd position) and then power up through your legs and jump straight up off the ground (4th position).

FIGURE 72 Burpee

a) 1st Position and 3rd Position

b) 2nd Position

c) 4th Position

Variations include:
- include a push-up in the plank position
- change the plank position to a sprawl (body is flat on the ground)
- add a tuck jump at the top
- omit the jump at the top

FAST FEET DRILLS

Start by standing in an athletic "ready" position, feet slightly wider than shoulder width, knees and hips slightly bent. Staying light on your toes, back straight and head up, alternate your feet up and down as fast as possible.

FIGURE 73 Fast Feet Drills

Variations include:

- add in sprawls—lay down flat on the floor, with your feet, hands, and stomach all making contact with the ground; jump back up to the ready stance as quickly as possible
- add in lateral (side to side) shuffle movement
- add in 90-degree turn jumps

MOUNTAIN CLIMBERS

Start in a plank position, arms extended underneath shoulders and feet out back behind you, so that your body is in a straight line. Without changing the posture of your lower back, alternate raising your knees toward your chest.

FIGURE 74 Mountain Climbers

BEAR CRAWL

Place your hands and feet on the floor without allowing your knees to touch the floor. Crawling forward, backward, and side to side keep your back in neutral position and your eyes facing forward.

FIGURE 75 Bear Crawl

BOX JUMPS

Stand with the box in front of you, feet shoulder-width apart, knees slightly bent. Jump up with two feet onto the box. Land with your entire foot on the box (for safety) and then stand up straight. Hop down and repeat.

FIGURE 76 Box Jumps

STEP UPS

Stand with box (or bench) in front of you. Step one foot up onto box, so that the entire foot is flat on the box. Power up through your leg so that you are standing up on top of the box, bringing your opposite foot up to touch the toe onto the box. Step back down carefully and repeat with the opposite foot.

FIGURE 77   Step Ups

 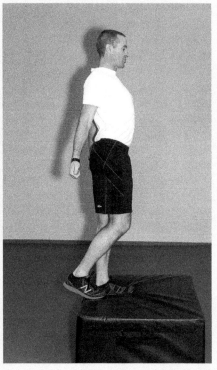

STAIR CLIMBING

Find a stairwell with approximately 50 or more stairs (an outdoor park or stadium would be ideal). Run up the stairs, touching every step. Return to the bottom as your rest interval and then repeat.

FIGURE 78   Stair Climbing

Variations include:

- run up every second step
- run up every third step
- jump up steps with a two-foot jump

AGILITY HURDLES

The hurdles used in the PARE test are 18 inches (45.7 cm) high and set 10 feet (approximately 3.05 m) from the cone and 10 feet apart from each other. To work on agility, line up 6 to 10 hurdles approximately 10 feet apart. While facing the hurdles, sprint forward as fast as possible, jumping over the hurdles and placing one foot in between each hurdle.

FIGURE 79 Agility Hurdles

Variations include:
- jump with two feet together over the hurdles
- jump with one foot (right and then left) over the hurdles

AGILITY LADDER DRILLS

Set up the agility ladder on the floor. There are many different types of ladder drills. Here are some examples:

- Forward running, high knees—run with high knees through the ladder, touching a foot down in every ladder space.

- Hopscotch—jump with two feet into a ladder space and then jump with both feet wide on the outsides of the ladder.

- Lateral running, high knees—step side to side through the ladder, one foot at a time, touching both feet down in every ladder space.

FIGURE 80   Agility Ladder Drills

NOTES:

_____

_____

_____

_____

_____

PYLON RUNNING DRILLS

Set up pylons in your space, either in a box format, straight line, or staggered line, each pylon about 5 to 10 m from each other. Run from each pylon to the next, staying low and moving fast.

FIGURE 81 Pylon Running Drills

Pylon drills variations can include:
- forward sprints
- backward sprints
- lateral sprints—side to side shuffle

FIGURE OF AN AGILITY CIRCUIT

Here is an example of an agility circuit, using some of the exercises from above, helping mimic components of the BFORs.

FIGURE 82 Example of an Agility Circuit

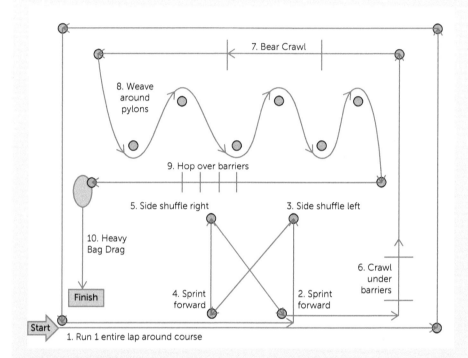

TRAINING FOR LÉGER'S 20-M SHUTTLE RUN

The value of cardiorespiratory fitness has been validated in many of the BFORs for law enforcement in Canada. The PREP, FITCO, A-PREP, and OPFA Standards use Léger's 20-m Shuttle Run as their aerobic assessment on criterion-based on-the-job tasks and aerobic fitness requirements.

To train to meet an acceptable level on the 20-m shuttle run, you should be doing cardiovascular training three to five times per week working at an intensity of 75 to 85 percent of your maximum heart rate.

You can use any of the following training regimes to help build up your aerobic capacity and speed required to achieve the test. Whichever training program you choose, it is vital that you are recording your runs in a logbook. At the end of the *Fit for Duty, Fit for Life* training guide there is a running log so that you can track your progress, and adjust your training when it is needed.

LEARNING TO RUN

Table 3 is an example of a learning-to-run training program. The emphasis of this program is to establish a cardiovascular base that focuses on time and distance with an intention to be able to run 5 kilometres by the end of 7 weeks. Once you successfully complete this program and can run the total time and distance without stopping, then you can focus on speed. For more tips on learning to run, go to Chapter 5 of the *Fitness and Lifestyle Management for Law Enforcement* textbook.

NOTES:

TABLE 3 Training to Run 5 km

	MONDAY	TUESDAY	WEDNESDAY	THURSDAY	FRIDAY	SATURDAY	SUNDAY
Run for 3 minutes/walk for 1 minute							
Week 1	Run/walk 30 minutes	Walk 30 minutes	Run/walk 30 minutes include HIIT	Walk 30 minutes	Rest	Run/walk 5 km (3.1 miles)	Rest or walk 30 minutes
Sprint Training (HIIT) 3–5 sprints once/week							
Run for 4 minutes/walk for 1 minute							
Week 2	Run/walk 30 minutes	Walk 30 minutes	Run/walk 30 minutes include HIIT	Walk 30 minutes	Rest	Run/walk 5.5 km (3.4 miles)	Rest or walk 30 minutes
Sprint Training (HIIT) 4–6 sprints once/week							
Run for 5 minutes/walk for 1 minute							
Week 3	Run/walk 30 minutes	Cross train 30 minutes	Run/walk 30 minutes include HIIT	Walk 30 minutes	Rest	Run/walk 2.4 km (1.5 mile) Time yourself	Rest or walk 30 minutes
Sprint Training (HIIT) 5–8 sprints (incorporate up to 3 times/week)							
Run for 6 minutes/walk for 1 minute							
Week 4	Run/walk 30 minutes	Cross train 30 minutes	Run/walk 30 minutes include HIIT	Walk 30 minutes include hill work	Rest	Run/walk 6 km (3.7 miles)	Rest or walk 30 minutes
Sprint Training (HIIT) 6–8 sprints, 3 times/week							
Run for 6 minutes/walk for 30 seconds							
Week 5	Run/walk 30 minutes	Cross train 30 minutes	Run/walk 30 minutes include HIIT	Walk 30 minutes	Rest	Run/walk 5.5 km (3.4 miles)	Rest or walk 30 minutes
Sprint Training (HIIT) 7–8 sprints, 3 times/week							
Run for 7 minutes/walk for 30 seconds or less							
Week 6	Run/walk 30 minutes	Cross train 30 minutes	Run/walk 30 minutes include HIIT	Walk 30 minutes	Rest	Run 2.4 km (1.5 mile) Time yourself	Rest or walk 30 minutes
Sprint Training (HIIT) 8 sprints, 3 times/week							
Run for 8 minutes/walk for 30 seconds or less							
Week 7	Run/walk 30 minutes	Cross train 30 minutes	Run/walk 30 minutes include HIIT	Walk 30 minutes	Rest	**Test day Run 5 km (3.1 miles)**	Rest or walk 30 minutes
Sprint Training (HIIT) 8 sprints							
Cross training includes biking, swimming, elliptical trainer. REMEMBER TO DO AT LEAST A 5 MINUTE WARM-UP AND A 5 MINUTE COOL-DOWN. It is important to take a rest day to prevent injuries.							

SOURCES: Denham, Feros, & O'Brien, 2015; Rebecca Finlay, personal communications, 2017; Galloway, 2008; RunningWithUs, n.d.

TRAINING WITH THE SHUTTLE RUN TRACK

Determine what is the maximum level you can obtain on the 20-m Léger Shuttle Run. When you can no longer run any further, stay in your lane and keep walking. When you feel that you can run again, do another 20 metres or more if possible. This way you will have a better understanding of the speed that you must work toward.

Some tips to training with the shuttle run track include:

a. Make sure that you are practising the actual test (you can find an MP3 of the test at https://www.applicanttesting.com/career-paths/police-constable/testing-information/140-police-constable-testing-information.html) and that you have measured out the distance using a tape measure so that you are running exactly 20 metres.

b. Make sure that you are pivoting on the 20-metre line. Don't make wide turns. You do not have to put two feet over the line.

c. Achieving 7.0 on the shuttle run test requires you to run 1,220 metres. Make sure that you are able to run this distance.

d. Another way to train would be to fast forward the track right to the stage that you want to achieve and run that full stage (1 minute in length) and then recover for one minute. You can repeat this as many times as necessary.

TRAINING ON A TREADMILL

The suggested training regime on the treadmill involves increasing the intensity every minute to simulate the shuttle run. The 20-m shuttle run pace starts at 8.5 kph and continues to increase by approximately 0.5 kph every full stage. The pace is 11.5 kph (7.15 mph) in the last minute to meet the stage 7.0.

Start with a 2 minute warm-up at a fast walking pace and then begin a light jog approximately 8.5 kph (5.3 mph). Each minute increase the pace slightly to mimic the shuttle run (see Table 4). When you can no longer run because you are at your maximum pace, slow the treadmill down to a walk and allow your heart rate to return to normal.

Please remember that this training will not simulate the 20-m shuttle run exactly, as you are not stopping, turning, and starting every 20 metres, nor are you pushing yourself forward as you would on the gym floor. Some individuals find that they can run for much longer on the treadmill than they can in the actual test. One thing that you can do to make the run more realistic is add at least a 2 percent incline to the treadmill.

TABLE 4 Training For the 20-m Shuttle Run

MINUTE	RUNNING SPEED	
	km/hr	mph
1	8.5	5.3
2	9.0	5.6
3	9.5	5.9
4	10.0	6.2
5	10.5	6.5
6	11.0	6.8
7	11.5	7.1
8	12.0	7.5
9	12.5	7.8
10	13.0	8.1
11	13.5	8.4
12	14.0	8.7
13	14.5	9
14	15	9.3
15	15.5	9.6
16	16	9.9
17	16.5	10.25
18	17	10.56
19	17.5	10.87
20	18	11.1

HIGH INTENSITY INTERVAL TRAINING (HIIT)

One way to improve your shuttle run performance is to do interval training. Make sure that you start with a 5 to 10 minute dynamic warm-up.

a. An example of a beginner HIIT program:

    i. 30 seconds at 50 percent MHR followed by

    ii. 20 seconds at 70 percent MHR followed by

    iii. 10 seconds at 90 percent MHR.

      Each set lasts 1 minute. Repeat for a minimum of 5 sets and maximum of 10 sets.

b. An example of an advanced HIIT program:

    i. 1 minute at 90 percent MHR followed by

    ii. 1 minute active recovery.

      Your goal is to repeat this 10 times, for a 20-minute workout.

c. An example of sprint training combined with a strength workout:

    i. Sprint for 1 to 2 minutes at 100 percent MHR.

    ii. Complete 2 or 3 weight exercises.

Repeat sprints as many times as necessary to accommodate your full strength workout.

CORE TRAINING

Core exercises train the muscles in your pelvis, lower back, hips, and abdomen to work together effectively. Core training is simply doing specific exercises to develop and strengthen these stabilizer muscles. This leads to better balance and stability, whether on the playing field or doing job-related tasks. If any of these core muscles are weakened, it could result in lower back pain or a protruding waistline.

The following exercises will assist you in training your core muscles.

CAT-COW STRETCH

Kneel on your hands and knees, with your knees in line with your feet and hands. Inhale and slowly round your spine toward the ceiling. Drop your head toward the floor and hold this position for a few seconds. Exhale and slowly bring your spine back to the starting position. Inhale and lift your chest and tailbone to the ceiling while curving your spine down toward the floor. Raise your head up and hold for a few seconds. Exhale and slowly bring your spine back to the starting position. Repeat 10 to 20 times.

FIGURE 83 Cat-Cow Stretch

MODIFIED CURL UP

Lie on your back with one knee bent and one leg flat on the floor. Place your hands under the lumbar spine to maintain a neutral spinal position. Brace your core, as you ever so slightly lift your head and shoulders off the ground. The movement should be very minimal. Hold for 5 seconds. Begin with 3 sets of 5 repetitions.

FIGURE 84　Modified Curl Up

NOTES:

BIRD DOG

Kneel on your hands and knees, making sure that your spine is neutral. Slowly, raise your right arm straight out in front of you while raising your left leg straight back. Try to keep your back completely still, so that there is no bending, twisting, or rotating of the spine. Hold this position for a few seconds. Slowly lower your limbs and bring your elbow and knee together under your body. Begin with 3 sets of 5 repetitions. Switch sides and repeat.

FIGURE 85 Bird Dog

SIDE BRIDGE

Lie on your side with your elbow directly under your shoulder and your chest facing the wall. Put your top foot in front of your bottom foot. Lift your hips up off the ground, so that you are supported by your elbow/forearm and your feet. Your body should be a straight line from your shoulders through your hips and to your feet. Your top arm can point toward the ceiling or rest on your top hip.

FIGURE 86   Side Bridge

NOTES:

HIP BRIDGE

Lie down on your back with your knees bent and feet flat on the floor, arms by your sides. Lift your hips as high up in the air as possible, by squeezing your gluteal muscles. Hold for 5 seconds and then lower down under control. Begin with 3 sets of 5 repetitions.

FIGURE 87 Hip Bridge

STIR THE POT

Kneel on the floor and place your forearms on a stability ball with your palms together. Push up onto your forearms and toes, so that your body is in a straight line and your core is braced. Move your arms on the ball to simulate stirring a big pot, while maintaining a stable plank. The size of the circle that you "stir" directly affects the intensity—a larger circle is more challenging. Begin with five to ten circles in one direction and then repeat in the other direction. Beginners can start on their knees.

FIGURE 88   Stir the Pot

DEAD BUGS

Lie on your back with your legs and hips bent at 90-degree angles, so your feet are held up in the air. Arms are fully extended above your chest area. Keeping your spine neutral, brace your core and lower your right arm and left leg. Bring them back up and switch sides (lower left arm and right leg).

FIGURE 89 Dead Bugs

ROLL OUTS

Leaning forward from your knees, grasp the ab roller on the ground directly below your shoulders. Keeping your spine neutral and your core braced, roll out as far as you can. Roll back up to the start position, keeping a straight alignment in your spine. Only go as far as you can while keeping your back straight.

FIGURE 90   Roll Outs

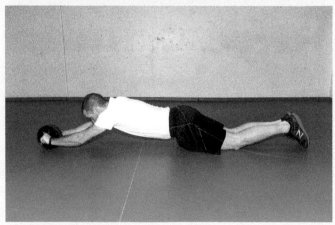

Variations include:
- use a stability ball
- use gliding discs
- do exercise from your toes

AROUND THE WORLD

Standing with your feet slightly wider than shoulder-width apart, grasp a medicine ball or weighted plate above your head. Keeping your core braced, start making full circles around your head with the weight. Start with a small circle and then increase to a bigger circle when you can do so without compromising your form. Change directions.

FIGURE 91 Around the World

WOOD CHOPPER

Choose your desired weight and set the handle on the cable at waist height. Stand with your left side facing the cable and grasp the handle with both hands, so that your right arm is reaching across your body. With your knees slightly bent, pull the cable handle across your body from left to right, pivoting on the balls of your feet. Keep your core braced and spine straight. Repeat on the other side.

FIGURE 92 Wood Chopper

PLANK

Refer to Push Exercises for explanation and photo.

SUITCASE CARRY

Refer to Victim Relocation for explanation and photo.

RESISTANCE TRAINING WORKOUT

In Chapter 5 and 6 of your *Fitness and Lifestyle Management for Law Enforcement* textbook, there are instructions and tips of how to put together your own workout based on your goals as well as examples of different programs. The textbook also includes resistance training workouts devised by the RCMP, the Ministry of Community Safety and Correctional Services, and the Canadian Forces for their specific BFORs. Here are two examples of resistance training workouts that incorporate a good balance of all of the exercises provided in this guidebook:

NOTES:

TABLE 5   Resistance Training Workouts

WORKOUT #1: CIRCUIT TRAINING	WORKOUT #2: SUPERSET TRAINING
Each circuit is to be done in succession, doing each exercise for 45 seconds. Repeat each circuit 2 to 3 times.	Each superset is to be done with no rest in between the exercises. Repeat each set 2 to 3 times.
Dynamic Warm-Up—10 minutes	
Circuit 1 • Sled Push • Cable Row • Squats (with shoulder press) • Forearm Plank • Burpees **Circuit 2** • Push-Ups • Upright Row • Farmer's Walk (with fat grips) • Stir The Pot • Tuck Jumps	**Superset 1** • Chest Fly • Bent Over Rows **Superset 2** • Leg Press • Calf Raises (on leg press machine) **Superset 3** • Front Raise (with a 5 second straight arm hold) • Overhead Triceps Extension **Superset 4** • Front Plank • Side Bridge • Hip Bridge **Superset 5** • Fast Feet Drills • Box Jumps
Cool Down—10 to 15 minutes, including stretching	

COOL DOWN

IMPORTANCE OF COOL DOWN AND STRETCHING

Similar to a warm-up, a cool-down should be an integral part of your workout at a slower pace and reduced intensity. The cool-down phase assures the appropriate return of blood to the heart, which in turn reduces the risk of dizziness and fainting (called syncope) that can occur if exercise is stopped suddenly. A cool-down should include approximately five minutes of low-intensity aerobic activity (e.g., walking or easy spinning on a bike) followed by approximately five to ten minutes of stretching.

Stretching improves your performance in some activities while decreasing your risk of muscle injury. Static, PNF, and fascial stretching are all great options for a cool-down routine. A common cue that individuals are not stretching at the end of their workouts are tight hamstring and achilles tendons, which can be seen in poor results for the sit and reach assessment (part of OPFA testing).

STATIC STRETCHING

The following are some examples of static-stretching exercises that you may want to include in your cool-down program. Remember to hold each stretch for at least 20–30 seconds.

NOTES:

SHOULDER STRETCH

Reach one arm across your body, parallel with your chest. With your opposite hand, grasp the straight arm behind the elbow and pull it tight to your body. Repeat with the other arm.

FIGURE 93   Shoulder Stretch

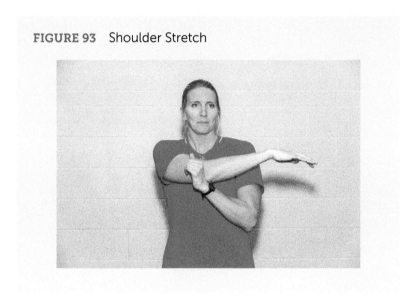

TRICEPS STRETCH

Bring one elbow up above your head and reach down your back as far as possible with that hand. With your other hand, grasp your elbow and gently pull it down behind the back of your head. Repeat with the other arm.

FIGURE 94   Triceps Stretch

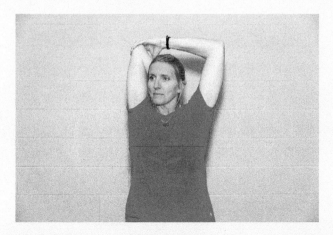

CHEST STRETCH

While clasping your hands behind your back, gently straighten your elbows and raise your arms as high as comfortably possible. Keep your back straight and stand in an upright position.

FIGURE 95 Chest Stretch

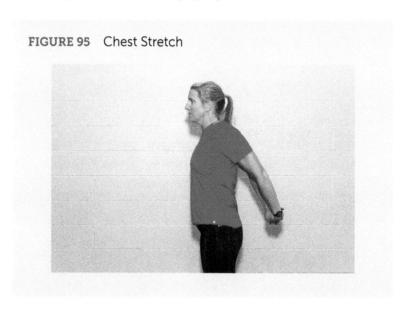

MID BACK STRETCH

While clasping your hands in front of your body, gently straighten your arms. Focus on rounding through your spine and separating your shoulder blades.

FIGURE 96 Mid Back Stretch

SIDE STRETCH

With hands above your head, lean to your right, stretching through your left side. Use your right hand to help pull your extended left arm further. Cross your left foot behind your right foot for an extended stretch. Repeat on your other side.

FIGURE 97 Side Stretch

ABDOMINALS AND BACK EXTENSION STRETCH

Lie facing the floor, with your forearms on the floor and hands under your chin area. Slowly straighten your arms and lift your chest off the ground, stretching through your abdominals and extending through your back.

FIGURE 98   Abdominals and Back Extension Stretch

QUADRICEPS STRETCH

Lie facing the floor and bend one leg up. Clasp your ankle with both hands and pull your heel to your buttocks while keeping your upper leg on the floor. To extend the stretch, flex your foot in your hand. Repeat with the other leg. This stretch can also be done lying on your side or standing.

FIGURE 99   Quadriceps Stretch

MODIFIED HURDLER STRETCH

Sit on the floor with your left leg straight out in front of you, toes pointing upward. Tuck your right foot in against your left leg. Bend forward from your hips, keeping your spine neutral, reaching forward with your upper body as far as possible. Repeat with the right leg.

FIGURE 100   Modified Hurdler Stretch

PIRIFORMIS STRETCH

Lie on your back with your knees bent. Lift one ankle up and place it across the opposite knee. Reach underneath the bottom leg and pull it up toward your chest. Repeat with the opposite leg.

FIGURE 101   Piriformis Stretch

ADDUCTOR STRETCH

Sit down and place the soles of your feet together. Pull your feet in close to your body. To enhance the stretch, gently push your knees down with your elbows.

FIGURE 102   Adductor Stretch

HIP FLEXOR STRETCH

Kneel in a semi-kneeling position (one knee down and the other in front at a 90-degree angle). Press your hips forward, stretching through the hip flexor of your kneeling leg. Repeat with the opposite leg.

FIGURE 103   Hip Flexor Stretch

CALF STRETCH

Stand an arm's length away from a wall and place one toe up against the wall. Lean toward the wall, by pushing off of your back foot. Repeat with opposite leg.

FIGURE 104 Calf Stretch

PNF STRETCHING

The following is an example of a partner-assisted proprioceptive neuro-muscular facilitation (PNF) stretch that you could add into your cool-down stretching program. The goal in a PNF stretch is to contract the muscle that you want to stretch and then passively relax it, while your partner assists in stretching it.

HAMSTRING STRETCH

Lie on your back, and put one leg straight up in the air (your partner can assist by keeping one hand in front of your knee to prevent it from bending). Then press your lifted leg into the hands of your partner for approximately 5 seconds, trying to push your leg down to the floor (they will actively push back, providing resistance). Then relax your leg and allow your partner to stretch it for you.

FIGURE 105   Hamstring Stretch

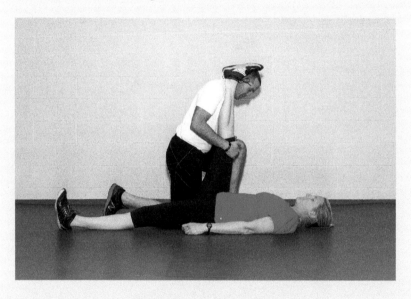

NOTES:

FASCIAL STRETCHING

The following photos are ways to stretch your fascia. Fascia is the fibrous connective tissue that wraps around and supports all of your muscles, bones, and organs. Using a foam roller and/or a hard small ball (e.g., lacrosse ball) can also help release these tissues. Try to hold each stretch for approximately 60 seconds.

FIGURE 106 Fascial Stretch

a) Fascial Stretch Upper Body and Side

b) Foam Roller

PLANNING NUTRITION AROUND YOUR WORKOUT

To get the maximum results from your workout, take time to plan your pre- and post-workout meals. Eating a balanced diet with proper nutrients throughout the day will set you up to have good energy going into a workout. Take time to fuel your body properly so that you are ready to exercise any time of day. Equally, after a workout it is important to replenish your energy stores. Eating the right nutrients soon after your workout rebuilds your glycogen stores and repairs your muscle proteins.

PRE-EXERCISE FUELLING

The basic goals of a pre-exercise meal/snack are as follows:

- to prevent weakness and fatigue, whether due to low blood sugar levels or inadequate muscles glycogen stores, during the event.
- to ward off hunger yet minimize gastrointestinal distress from eating.
- to guarantee optimal hydration.
- increase muscle performance, muscle growth, and muscle recovery.

Aim to eat 1.5 to 2 hours before working out. The ideal pre-sport meal has the following characteristics:

- Approximately 300 to 500 calories.
- High in carbohydrates (primarily complex carbohydrates).
- Moderate in protein (important for increased muscle performance, growth, and recovery).
- Low in fat (important for longer and moderate to low intensity exercises).
- Low in fibre.
- Contains fluids.
- Made up of familiar, well-tolerated foods.

Pre-exercise meals and snacks can include:

- chicken sandwich on whole grain bread and side salad
- egg omelette and whole grain toast topped with avocado spread and a cup of fruit

- fish, brown rice, and roasted vegetables
- oatmeal with nuts and dried fruit
- a small piece of fruit, such as apple, pear, or banana, with nut butter
- yogurt with granola and fresh fruit
- fruit smoothies that include fresh vegetables, flax seeds, and a small amount of protein (at least 2 hours before)
- hard-boiled eggs.

Remember to hydrate before exercising; at least 600 millilitres (20 fluid oz.) at least 2 hours before exercise and 250 to 500 millilitres (12 to 20 fluid oz.) 10 to 15 minutes before exercise.

DURING-EXERCISE FUELLING

If your workout lasts less than 1 hour, you don't need to replenish your nutrients, but you do need to stay hydrated. ACSM guidelines (2007) recommend drinking 3 to 8 ounces (90 ml to 240 ml) of water every 15 to 20 minutes when exercising less than 60 minutes.

If your workout does last longer than 1 hour, try to consume 50 to 100 calories every half hour. The fuel should be simple, easily digestible carbohydrates (30 to 60 grams of carbohydrates) that the body needs to maintain energy and prevent fatigue (Hacker-Thompson, 2016).

Examples of quick digestible snacks include:

- energy gels
- bananas
- oranges
- honey
- energy bars.

ACSM guidelines (2007) recommend drinking 3 to 8 ounces (90 ml to 240 ml) of a sports drink that contains 5 to 8 percent carbohydrates and electrolytes. Participants who find that sports drinks irritate the stomach can water them down. Keep in mind that these snacks only provide enough calories to keep going; they don't replace the calories you burn.

POST-EXERCISE FUELLING

After your workout, you should replace your energy deficit of carbohydrates and proteins as quickly as you can, ideally within 20 to 60 minutes for efficient storage of calories for energy and recovery. Proposed benefits include:

- improved recovery
- decreased muscle soreness
- increased ability to build muscle
- improved immune function
- improved bone mass
- improved ability to use body fat.

Combining protein and carbohydrates can nearly double the insulin response, resulting in more glycogen being stored, and enabling muscles to repair. It is recommended that you consume 0.3 to 0.6 grams of carbohydrates for each half-kilogram of body weight (for example, a person who weighs 70 kg would need 42 to 84 grams). Try to choose a snack with 300 to 400 calories containing an optimal ratio of carbohydrates to protein (ACSM suggests 2:1 ratio for short, low- to medium-intensity or 3:1 in long, high-intensity workouts (Hacker-Thompson, 2016)).

Some people can't easily consume whole foods immediately after exercise. Consuming a liquid form of easy digestable carbohydrates (e.g., maltodextrin, dextrose, glucose, etc.) and protein (e.g., protein hydrolysates or isolates) results in rapid digestion and absorption and is better tolerated after workouts. An example of a nutritional drink that is a good blend of carbohydrates and protein is 1 percent chocolate milk, which gives you 26 grams of carbohydrates and 8 grams of protein.

Simple post-workout meals/snacks include:

- chicken and brown rice
- yogurt and almonds
- a protein shake with a banana
- peanut butter and banana on a rice cake
- hummus and pita
- tuna salad on whole wheat bread
- turkey slices with cheese and apples.

Also, remember to hydrate after a workout. Drinking 600 to 700 millilitres (20 to 24 fluid oz.) for every half kilogram (1 lb.) of weight lost during exercise is the common guideline.

ONTARIO POLICE FITNESS AWARD (OPFA)

The Police Fitness Personnel of Ontario (PFPO) was founded in 1988 by a working partnership of subject matter experts in police fitness and occupational sciences employed by national, provincial, and municipal police services. The primary aim of the PFPO was to provide human resources support for police operations in physical fitness programming and recruit selection and training. This led to training for officers to implement a basic fitness assessment that could be implemented by all police services in the province of Ontario.

For over 30 years the Ontario Police Fitness Award (OPFA) Program is an example of a healthy public policy for a provincial incentive program developed to motivate Ontario police officers and police service employees to remain physically fit and be recognized with a fitness pin award throughout their careers. The policing services division of the Ministry of Community Safety and Correctional Services and the Ontario Association of Chiefs of Police sanction the OPFA program. The program has been so successful in Ontario that other law enforcement services have requested the use of the program. The PFPO are working at making it a National Law Enforcement Fitness Award.

There are four components that combine to have a maximum score of 100 and you must achieve 75 marks overall to pass. The fitness assessments and grading for the OPFA Fitness Standards include:

Push-Ups	(____/20)
Core Endurance	(____/20)
Trunk Forward Flexion	(____/10)
1.5-Mile Run or Leger 20-m Shuttle Run	(____/50)
Total Score	(____/100)

Tables and descriptions of the fitness assessments are on the following pages and are adapted from the OPFA standards. Each table provides benchmarks that allow you to score your performance and gauge your improvement as you work toward your goal of meeting law enforcement fitness standards.

PUSH-UPS

Push-ups are a test of muscular endurance, which is defined as the ability of a muscle to perform repeated contractions over a period of time. The push-ups are to be performed consecutively and without a time limit. The test is terminated when the participant has completed as many push-ups as possible, or when their form deviates too much from the correct procedure.

In many cases, lack of compliance with the OPFA protocol (that is, arching the back on a push-up, trying to reach the floor by straining your neck only, not going down far enough, moving hands farther apart, failing to keep the upper body in a straight line, not going to full extension, forcibly straining, or pausing for too long between push-ups) terminates the test. If the person corrects the technique, the inappropriate push-up is not counted, and the participant can continue until he or she deviates in two consecutive repetitions.

It is not acceptable for either males or females to have their feet against a wall or for a mat to be placed under their chin.

NOTES:

MALE PROTOCOL

The participant lies on his stomach with legs together. His hands, pointing forward, are positioned under the shoulders. To begin, the participant pushes up from the mat by fully straightening the elbows to full extension, using the toes as the pivotal point. The upper body must be kept in a straight line. The participant returns to the starting position, chin to the mat. Neither the stomach nor the thighs should touch the mat.

FIGURE 107 Male Push-Ups

FEMALE PROTOCOL

The participant lies on her stomach with legs together. Her hands, pointing forward, are positioned under the shoulders. She then pushes up from the mat by fully straightening the elbows, using the knees as the pivot point. Flexing at the elbows, she lowers the body, maintaining a neutral spine (body held in a straight line). The participant returns to the starting position with only the chin to the mat. The stomach and hips cannot touch the mat and the hip should not be flexed. The participant must have the lower leg remain in contact with the mat, ankles plantar-flexed.

FIGURE 108 Female Push-Ups

TABLE 6 Push-ups Results and Scores, Male and Female

SCORE	AGE									
	20–29		30–39		40–49		50–59		60+	
	Male	Female	Male	Female	Male	Female	Male	Female	Male	Female
20	49+	38+	37+	37+	31+	33+	29+	31+	28+	31+
19	48	37	36	36	30	32	28	30	25–27	30
18	36–47	30–36	30–35	27–35	22–29	24–31	21–27	21–29	18–24	17–29
17	32–35	24–29	25–29	22–26	20–21	20–23	15–20	15–20	13–17	13–16
16	29–31	21–23	22–24	20–21	17–19	15–19	13–14	12–14	11–12	12
15	27–28	20	21	17–19	16	14	12	11	10	10–11
14	25–26	18–19	20	16	15	13	11	10	10	9
12	24	16–17	19	14–15	13–14	12	10	9	9	6–8
10	21–23	14–15	16–18	12–13	12	10–11	9	5–8	7–8	4–5
8	18–20	11–13	14–15	10–11	10–11	7–9	7–8	3–4	6	2–3
6	16–17	9–10	11–13	7–9	8–9	4–6	5–6	1–2	4–5	1
4	11–15	5–8	8–10	4–6	5–7	2–3	4	—	2–3	—
2	10	4	7	3	4	1	3	—	1	—
0	≤9	≤3	≤6	≤2	≤3	0	≤2	0	0	0

SOURCE: PFPO, 2017.

CORE ENDURANCE (MODIFIED BIERING-SORENSEN BACK EXTENSION TEST)

This assessment is for those participants who are asymptomatic and pass the pre-screening for having no back problems. The participant must have filled out his or her PAR-Q+ and must have no restrictions.

PRE-SCREENING

The participant lies face down on a mat and performs a straight leg extension with the right leg and then the left, with arms outstretched in front. If there is no pain, then he or she is told to repeat the same movements with the opposing arm outstretched and lifted at the same time. Then the participant returns to the starting position. If no pain is indicated, he or she proceeds to the test.

FIGURE 109   Pre-Screening for Core Endurance

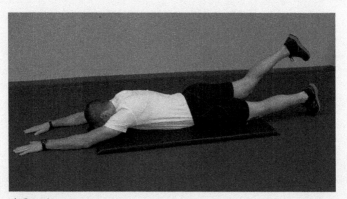

a) One Leg

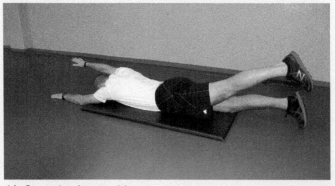

b) Opposite Arm and Leg

PROTOCOL

Note: Standards are based on the modified Biering-Sorensen back assessment.

The participant lies face down on top of the bench with the lower body on the bench. The iliac crest is positioned at the edge of the bench (your appraiser will ensure that it is in the right location). The participant needs to be secured by either straps or a partner with their arms supporting their upper body until the test begins (Figure 110). Before starting the test, the participant is told to use core muscles throughout the test. A towel may be placed under the ankles to add support and keep feet in a neutral position.

FIGURE 110   Starting Position for Core Endurance

Once the participant is secured, he or she is instructed to raise the upper body until it is parallel with the lower body. The participant's arms are placed across their chest with the hands on the opposing shoulders. The participant may not grab on to their shirt or allow their hands to leave their shoulders. The entire body forms one straight line, with no rotation, arching, or lateral shifting. The neck is straight and neutral. The participant stays in this position for as long as possible to a maximum of 180 seconds. Participants are allowed one warning to reposition themselves if they drop below parallel. The test is terminated when the participant puts their hands to the ground, or drops below parallel twice.

The score is based on the number of seconds that the test is performed.

FIGURE 111   Core Endurance

a) Correct Position

b) Incorrect Position

TABLE 7 Biering-Sorensen Back Assessment: Core Endurance Test Results and Scores, Male and Female

SCORE	AGE									
	20–29		30–39		40–49		50–59		60+	
	Male	Female	Male	Female	Male	Female	Male	Female	Male	Female
20	3:00	3:00	3:00	3:00	2:45–3:00	3:00	2:41–3:00	2:36–3:00	2:00–3:00	2:29–3:00
19	2:50–2:59	2:51–2:59	2:43–2:59	2:51–2:59	2:30–2:44	2:46–2:59	2:21–2:40	2:13–2:35	1:53–1:59	2:00–2:28
18	2:40–2:49	2:41–2:50	2:27–2:42	2:43–2:50	2:10–2:29	2:33–2:45	2:00–2:20	1:50–2:12	1:44–1:52	1:31–1:59
17	2:31–2:39	2:32–2:40	2:13–2:26	2:36–2:42	1:55–2:09	2:20–2:32	1:50–1:59	1:38–1:49	1:35–1:43	1:14–1:30
16	2:21–2:30	2:24–2:31	2:01–2:12	2:28–2:35	1:39–1:54	2:07–2:19	1:40–1:49	1:26–1:37	1:26–1:34	0:57–1:13
15	2:12–2:20	2:15–2:23	1:48–2:00	2:20–2:27	1:23–1:38	1:54–2:06	1:27–1:39	1:14–1:25	1:17–1:25	0:39–0:56
14	2:00–2:11	2:04–2:14	1:42–1:47	2:01–2:19	1:19–1:22	1:43–1:53	1:17–1:26	1:06–1:13	1:09–1:16	0:33–0:38
12	1:50–1:59	1:53–2:03	1:36–1:41	2:01–2:10	1:14–1:18	1:32–1:42	1:06–1:16	0:56–1:05	1:01–1:08	0:26–0:32
10	1:39–1:49	1:42–1:52	1:31–1:34	1:52–2:00	1:10–1:13	1:20–1:31	0:54–1:05	0:47–0:55	0:52–1:00	0:19–0:25
8	1:35–1:38	1:30–1:41	1:19–1:30	1:35–1:51	0:59–1:09	1:08–1:19	0:43–0:53	0:37–0:46	0:42–0:51	0:15–0:18
6	1:30–1:34	1:18–1:29	1:07–1:18	1:18–1:34	0:45–0:58	0:55–1:07	0:31–0:42	0:26–0:36	0:30–0:41	0:11–0:14
4	1:26–1:29	1:06–1:17	0:56–1:06	1:01–1:17	0:32–0:44	0:42–0:54	0:20–0:30	0:15–0:25	0:20–0:29	0:06–0:10
2	≤1:25	≤1:05	≤0:55	≤1:00	≤0:31	≤0:41	≤0:19	≤0:14	≤0:19	≤0:05
0					DID NOT ATTEMPT					

SOURCE: PFPO, 2017.

TRUNK FORWARD FLEXION (SIT AND REACH)

The trunk forward flexion test measures the flexibility of the hamstring and lower back muscles. Flexibility depends upon the elasticity of the muscles, tendons, and ligaments, and is the ability to bend without injury. The trunk forward flexion test was chosen as an assessment that could show that restriction in the pelvis and tight hamstring muscles were associated with risk of low back pain.

Participants warm up for this test by performing slow stretching movements before the actual measurements are taken. One of the recommended warm-up stretches includes the modified hurdler stretch (see Figure 100).

NOTES:

_____

_____

_____

_____

_____

_____

_____

_____

_____

_____

_____

PROTOCOL

Participants, without shoes, sit with legs fully extended and the soles of the feet placed flat against the flexometer. Keeping the knees fully extended, arms evenly stretched, and palms down, participants bend and reach forward (without bouncing or jerking). The position of maximum flexion must be held for approximately 2 seconds. Participants are advised to lower their head during the motion to maximize the distance reached. Each participant is allowed two attempts, with the higher result scored.

FIGURE 112   Trunk Forward Flexion

a) Start Position

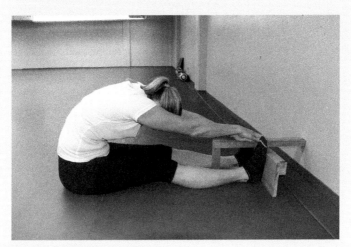

b) End Position

TABLE 8 Trunk Forward Flexion Results and Scores, Male and Female

SCORE	AGE									
	20–29		30–39		40–49		50–59		60+	
	Male	Female	Male	Female	Male	Female	Male	Female	Male	Female
10	45+	46+	44+	46+	41+	44+	42+	44+	45+	41+
9.5	44–44.5	45–45.5	42.5–43.5	45–45.5	39–40.5	42–43.5	40–41.5	42–43.5	40–44.5	39–40.5
9	40–43.5	41–44.5	38–42	41–44.5	37–38.5	40–41.5	37–39.5	40–41.5	36–39.5	37–38.5
8.5	37–39.5	39–40.5	35–37.5	38–40.5	35–36.5	38–39.5	35–36.5	38–39.5	32–35.5	35–36.5
8	34–36.5	37–38.5	33–34.5	36–37.5	32–34.5	36–37.6	33–34.5	36–37.5	29–31.5	33–34.5
7.5	33–33.5	36–36.5	32–32.5	35–35.5	29–31.5	34–35.5	30–32.5	34–35.5	26–28.5	31–32.5
7	32–32.5	35–35.5	31–31.5	34–34.5	27–28.5	32–33.5	27–29.5	32–33.5	24–25.5	29–30.5
6	31–31.5	34–34.5	29–30.5	33–33.5	25–26.5	29–31.5	25–26.5	30–31.5	22–23.5	27–28.5
5	29–30.5	32–33.5	27–28.5	31–32.5	23–24.5	26–28.5	22–24.5	28–2.59	18–21.5	25–26.5
4	26–28.5	29–31.5	24–26.5	28–30.5	20–22.5	24–25.5	18–21.5	25–27.5	16–17.5	23–24.5
3	23–25.5	26–28.5	21–23.5	25–27.5	16–19.5	22–23.5	15–17.5	22–24.5	14–15.5	21–22.5
2	18–22.5	22–25.5	17–20.5	21–24.5	12–15.5	19–21.5	12–14.5	19–21.5	11–13.5	18–20.5
1	≤17	≤21.5	≤16.5	≤20.5	≤11.5	≤18.5	≤11.5	≤18.5	≤10.5	≤17.5
0	DID NOT ATTEMPT									

SOURCE: PFPO, 2017.

1.5-MILE (2.4-KM) RUN

The 1.5-mile (2.4-km) run is a test of aerobic fitness and cardiovascular endurance. It tests the combined efficiency of the lungs, heart, bloodstream, and local muscles in getting oxygen to the muscles and putting them to work. The test is appropriate for those individuals who have engaged in vigorous physical activity within the past six months. Many specialized units use this protocol due to the demands of the job (TRUE, ERT, Canine, etc.).

PROTOCOL

Participants are required to cover an accurately measured 1.5-mile distance in as short a time as possible.

At the start, all participants will line up behind the starting line. On the command "Go" the clock is started and they are asked to begin running at their own pace. The total time to complete the course is recorded and scored. If at any point you can no longer run, you may walk or stop. If you are showing signs of fatigue (such as wobbling, nausea, trouble breathing) you will be encouraged to stop.

Prior to starting, you should complete at least a 5-minute dynamic warm-up that could include a walk or light jog, followed by some basic dynamic stretching exercises. At the completion of the timed run, you will be required to continue a cool-down walk for at least 5 to 10 minutes.

NOTES:

TABLE 9   1.5-Mile Run Results and Scores, Male and Female

SCORE	20–29		30–34		35–39		40–59		50+	
	Male	*Female*	*Male*	*Female*	*Male*	*Female*	*Male*	*Female*	*Male*	*Female*
50	≤9:00	≤10:35	≤9:20	≤11:00	≤10:06	≤11:53	≤10:54	≤13:04	≤11:59	≤14:22
47.5	9:01–9:30	10:36–11:10	9:21–9:50	11:01–11:35	10:07–10:37	11:54–12:31	10:55–11:41	13:05–13:46	12:00–12:51	14:23–15:08
45	9:31–10:00	11:11–11:52	9:51–10:20	11:36–12:10	10:38–11:10	12:32–13:08	11:42–12:17	13:47–14:27	12:52–13:31	15:09–15:53
42.5	10:01–10:30	11:53–12:34	10:21–10:50	12:11–12:45	11:11–11:42	13:09–13:46	12:18–12:52	14:28–15:08	13:32–14:07	15:54–16:38
40	10:31–10:56	12:35–13:00	10:51–11:20	12:46–13:20	11:43–12:14	13:47–14:24	12:53–13:28	15:09–15:50	14:08–14:49	16:39–17:25
37.5	10:57–11:22	13:01–13:26	11:21–11:50	13:21–13:55	12:15–12:47	14:25–15:02	13:29–14:04	15:51–16:32	14:50–15:28	17:26–18:11
35	11:23–11:46	13:27–13:42	11:51–12:20	13:56–14:30	12:48–13:19	15:03–15:40	14:05–14:39	16:33–17:14	15:29–16:07	18:12–18:57
30	11:47–12:10	13:43–13:57	12:21–12:50	1431–15:05	13:20–13:52	15:41–16:17	14:40–15:15	17:15–17:55	16:08–16:47	18:58–19:42
25	12:11–12:35	13:58–14:12	12:51–13:20	15:06–15:40	13:53–14:24	16:18–16:55	15:16–15:50	17:56–18:21	16:48–17:25	19:43–20:11
20	12:36–12:59	14:13–14:27	13:21–13:50	15:41–16:15	14:25–14:56	16:56–17:33	15:51–16:26	18:22–19:18	17:26–18:05	20:12–21:14
15	13:00–13:30	14:28–14:42	13:51–14:20	16:16–16:50	14:57–15:29	17:34–18:11	16:27–17:02	19:19–20:06	18:06–18:44	21:15–22:00
10	13:31–14:00	14:43–14:57	14:21–14:50	16:51–17:25	15:30–16:01	18:12–18:29	17:03–17:37	20:07–20:41	18:45–19:23	22:01–22:45
5	14:01–14:30	14:58–15:12	14:51–15:20	17:26–18:00	16:02–16:34	18:50–19:26	17:38–18:13	20:42–21:22	19:24–20:02	22:46–23:30
0						DID NOT ATTEMPT OR FAILED TO MEET MINIMUM STANDARD TIME				

SOURCE: PFPO, 2017.

MAXIMAL LÉGER 20-METRE SHUTTLE RUN

This test is an evaluation of aerobic fitness. A warm-up is included as part of the test and only the last portion of the test may require maximal effort. The objective is to follow the progressively faster pace over a 20-metre course.

PROTOCOL

At every signal you must have reached the next 20-metre line at each end marked by the pylons. One foot must be on or over the line, then, upon hearing the signal, reverse your direction and arrive at the other line in time for the next signal. To turn, *pivot* on the ball of your foot. Do not make wide turns. At the start it will be very slow, so you may reach the line with time to spare. However, you must wait for the signal before you leave. *Two metres* in front of the end lines are *warning lines*.

You will be cautioned clearly when you miss the first warning line. However, you must still reach the end line before starting the next leg. If you miss the warning line at one end but you make it to the other end, the warnings start over. If twice in a row you have not crossed the warning line when the signal sounds, the last stage announced on the tape is the last completed stage and you must exit at the end of your lane. *The two warnings must be consecutive.* Do not cross into another person's lane.

If you experience abnormal changes in blood pressure, dizziness/fainting, irregular heart rhythm, or chest pain stop the test immediately and advise one of the appraisers.

FIGURE 113 Shuttle Run

TABLE 10 OPFA Result Scores for 20-m Shuttle Run, Male and Female

SCORE	20–29 Male	20–29 Female	30–34 Male	30–34 Female	35–39 Male	35–39 Female	40–49 Male	40–49 Female	50+ Male	50+ Female
50	≥12	≥9.5	≥11.5	≥9	≥10.5	≥8	≥9	≥6.5	≥7.5	≥5.5
47.5	11.5	9	11	8–8.5	10	7.5	8–8.5	6	7	5
45	11	8–8.5	10.5	7.5	9–9.5	7	7.5	5–5.5	6.5	4.5
42.5	10–10.5	7.5	9.5–10	7	8–8.5	6–6.5	7	4.5	5.5–6	4
40	9–9.5	7	8.5–9	6.5	7.5	5.5	6–6.5	4	5	3.5
37.5	8.5	6.5	8	6	7	5	5.5	3.5	4.5	2.5-3
35	8	6.0	7.5	5	6.5	4.5	5	3	4	2
30	7.5	5.5	7	4.5	6	4	4.5	2.5	3.5	1.5
25	7	5	6.5	4	5.5	3.5	4	2	3	1
20	6.5	4.5	6	3.5	5	3	3.5	1.5	2.5	0.5
15	6	4.0	5.5	3	4.5	2.5	3	1	2	–
10	5.5	3.5	5	2.5	4	2	2.5	0.5	1.5	–
5	5	3	4.5	2	3	1.5	2.0	–	1	–
0	DID NOT ATTEMPT OR FAILED TO MEET MINIMUM SCORE									

SOURCE: PFPO, 2017.

ADDITIONAL FITNESS STANDARDS

Various fitness assessments may provide feedback on the progress of your goals. They can also assist you with key information to help you create or modify your fitness program. The bench press tests upper body strength, the chin-ups test muscular endurance, and the leg press tests leg power. Protocols and standards for the bench press, chin-ups, and leg press have been included below.

BENCH PRESS

The bench press—with standard weights pre-set for a selectorized plate machine—provides an indication of upper-body strength. Based on an old universal machine, this test has been adopted for a Smith machine (for safety and time restraints), although either can be used.

Table 11 provides the scale from an old universal and the comparison weight on a Smith machine. Each weight is considered a plate on the scoring sheet. Your 100 percent body weight is the weight closest to your body weight.

The bench press chart in Table 12 shows the score that you earn when you lift a certain amount of weight. For example, if you lift five plates below your body weight, you receive the score of 10; if you lift your full body weight, your score is 20; if you lift one plate below your body weight, you score 18; and so on.

NOTES:

TABLE 11 Comparison of Weight Between Universal Machine (with Pre-Determined Weight) and Comparable Weights on Smith Machine

BENCH PRESS SCALE (LBS)	SMITH MACHINE (LBS)
330	330
296	300
279	280
265	265
248	250
231	230
215	215
198	200
182	180
165	165
149	150
132	130
115	115
100	100
80	80
66	65
50	50

* Note: Each weight is considered a plate. Your 100% body weight is the weight closest to your body weight.

SOURCE: Adapted with permission. Marian Reeves. Peel Regional Police Service 2017 recruit standards. 2017 Brampton, Ontario, Peel Regional Police.

TABLE 12 Scoring for Bench Press

SCORE (/20)	AGE 20–29		AGE 30–39	
	Male	*Female*	*Male*	*Female*
+1	+4 plates	+3plates	+4 plates	+3 plates
+1	+2 plates	+2 plates	+2 plates	+1 plates
20	100% body wt.	100% body wt.	100% body wt.	100% body wt.
18	−1 plate	−1 plate	−1 plate	−1 plate
16	−2 plates	−2 plates	−2 plates	−2 plates
14	−3 plates	−3 plates	−3 plates	−3 plates
12	−4 plates	−4 plates	−4 plates	−4 plates
10	−5 plates	−5 plates	−5 plates	−5 plates
8	−6 plates	−6 plates	−6 plates	−6 plates
6	−7 plates	−7 plates	−7 plates	−7 plates
4	−8 plates	−8 plates	−8 plates	−8 plates
2	−9 plates	−9 plates	−9 plates	−9 plates
0	Did not attempt			

SOURCE: Adapted with permission. Marian Reeves. Peel Regional Police Service 2017 recruit standards. 2017 Brampton, Ontario, Peel Regional Police.

PROTOCOL

This test requires the applicant to lie supine on a flat bench with knees bent up and feet flat on the bench or legs bent at the knees such that the feet are in contact with the ground. Head and back must maintain contact with the bench. Assistance is given to the applicant to lift the chosen weight until he or she has arms fully extended. When the applicant indicates readiness, he or she will flex the arms, bringing the weight down until an angle of 90 degrees at the elbow is achieved at which time the weight will then be pressed back to the starting position (full extension). Remember not to lift your feet from planted position, lift your head off the bench, or arch your back.

One maximum repetition only is required at the weight chosen by the applicant. You are permitted a total of three attempts ONLY if you are successful on the previous lift. Do not start at your maximum weight. Termination happens when you miss one weight. Since you only have a maximum of three attempts, start at a warm-up weight and then move to the weight you believe you can bench.

FIGURE 114 Bench Press Set up

a) Feet Up

b) Feet Down

FIGURE 115 Bench Press

a) Flexion Position

b) Extension Position

CHIN-UPS

This test requires a functional range of flexibility, good elbow flexor strength, and back shoulder girdle strength.

PROTOCOL

The participant is required to pull him- or herself off the ground by fully flexing the arms. The chin must be brought up above the level of the bar and the body is lowered until the angle at the elbow joint is at least 90 degrees. The hands grip the bar in an underneath grip position while the movement is repeated continually over a period of 30 seconds.

FIGURE 116 Chin-Up

a) Starting Position   b) 90 Degrees

TABLE 13 Chin-Ups Results and Scores, Male and Female

SCORE (OUT OF 10)	NUMBER OF CHIN-UPS COMPLETED IN 30 SECONDS			
	Age 20–29		Age 30–39	
	Males	*Females*	*Males*	*Females*
+1	30	20	27	16
+1	24	15	22	13
10	18	10	17	10
9	17	9	16	9
8	16	8	15	8
7	15	7	14	7
6	14	6	13	6
5	13	5	12	5
4	12	4	11	4
3	11	3	10	3
2	10	2	9	2
1	9	1	8	1

SOURCE: Adapted with permission from Reeves, M. (2017). Peel Regional Police recruit fitness standards. Brampton, ON: Peel Regional Police Service.

LEG PRESS

PROTOCOL

Using a universal leg press, you will have three attempts to press your maximum weight as long as you are successful at each attempt (like bench press). Hands grasp the seat's handle with back straight and legs parallel to the floor. Feet are on machine rests with toes pointed slightly outward and the pressure is on the balls and heels of the feet. Extend your legs with knees partially locked. Stop momentarily and then the weight is to be lowered slowly back to the start position. You should not arch or twist your body.

FIGURE 117 Leg Press

a) Starting Position

b) Extension Position

SCORING FOR LEG PRESS

The grading for the 1-RM leg press is a based on McArdle, Katch, and Katch (2000) reference values for 1-RM leg press relative to body weight. A perfect score of 20/20 would be a 1-RM leg press that is 2.5 times your body weight.

Take your 1-RM weight from the leg press and *divide it* by 2.5 × *your body weight* and then multiple by *20* for a mark out of *20*.

$$Mark = 1\text{-}RM/(2.5 \times Body\ Wt.) \times 20$$

So, for example, if you leg press *300 lb.* and you weigh *150 lb.,* your mark would be

$$Mark = 300/(2.5 \times 150) \times 20$$
$$Mark = 300/375 \times 20$$
$$Mark = 16/20$$

NOTES:

_____

_____

_____

_____

_____

_____

_____

_____

_____

_____

_____

_____

_____

REFERENCES

Alberta Solicitor General and Public Safety. (2008). Fit to serve: Preparing for the A-PREP: Alberta physical readiness evaluation for police. Toronto: Queen's Printer of Ontario. Retrieved from http://www.calgary.ca/cps/ Documents/application-forms/fit-to-serve.pdf?noredirect=1

Alberta Solicitor General and Public Security. (n.d.). COPAT correctional officer's physical abilities test. Retrieved from https://www.solgps.alberta.ca/ careers/Publications/COPAT Requirements.pdf

American College of Sports Medicine (ACSM). (2007). Exercise and fluid replacement. *Medicine & Science in Sports & Exercise, 39*(2), 377–390. doi: 10.1249/mss.0b013e31802ca597

Bushman, B. (Ed.) (2017). *American College of Sports Medicine's complete guideline to fitness and health* (2nd ed.). Champaign IL: Human Kinetics.

Canadian Forces Morale and Welfare Services (CFMWS). (2016). *FORCE operation manual* (2nd ed.). Retrieved from https://www.cfmws.com/en/ AboutUs/PSP/DFIT/Fitness/FORCEprogram/Pages/FORCE-Operations -Manual-2nd-Edition.aspx

Canadian Society for Exercise Physiology (CSEP). (2011). Canadian physical activity guidelines for adults 18–64 years. Retrieved from http://www.csep .ca/en/guidelines/guidelines-for-other-age-groups

Denham, J., Feros, S.A., & O'Brien, B.J. (2015). Four weeks of sprint interval training improves 5-km run performance. Journal of Strength and Conditioning Research, 29(8), 2137–2141.

Galloway, J. (2008). Galloway's 5k/10k running (2nd ed.). Aachen, Germany: Meyer & Meyer Sport.

Garber, C.E., Blissmer, B., Deschenes, M.R., Franklin, B.A., Lamonte, M.J., Lee, I.M., Nieman, D.C., Swain, D.P., American College of Sports Medicine. (2011). American College of Sports Medicine position stand. Quantity and quality of exercise for developing and maintaining cardiorespiratory, musculoskeletal, and neuromotor fitness in apparently healthy adults: Guidance for prescribing exercise. *Medicine & Science in Sports & Exercise 43*(7):1334–59. doi: 10.1249/MSS.0b013e318213fefb

Gledhill, N., & Jamnik, R. (2015). *Technical guide: Physical readiness evaluation for police constable applicants (PREP)*. Ontario Association of Chiefs of Police Constable Selection System. Toronto: Ontario Ministry of Community Safety and Correctional Services.

Hacker-Thompson, A. (2016). Preventing the "low fuel light" in endurance exercise. ACSM Public Information Article. Retrieved from http://www .acsm.org/public-information/articles/2016/10/07/preventing-the-low-fuel -light-in-endurance-exercise

Jamnik, V.K., Thomas, S.G., Burr, J.F., & Gledhill, N. (2010). Construction, validation, and derivation of performance standards for a fitness test for correctional officer applicants. *Applied Physiology, Nutrition, and Metabolism, 35,* 59–70. doi: 10.1139/H09-122

Law Enforcement Physical Ability Testing Inc. (LEPAT). (2017a). Correctional officer's physical abilities test (COPAT) layout. Retrieved from http://www.lepat.com/files/Image/lepat_copat_course.png

Law Enforcement Physical Ability Testing Inc. (LEPAT). (2017b) Police officer's physical abilities test (POPAT) layout. Retrieved from http://www .lepat.com/files/Image/lepat_popat_course.png

Léger, L.A., & Lambert, J. (1982). A maximal multistage 20-m shuttle run test to predict VO$_2$ max. *European Journal of Applied Physiology, 49,* 1–5.

McArdle, W.D., Katch, F.I., & Katch, V.L. (2000). *Essentials of exercise physiology* (2nd ed.). Philadelphia: Lippincott Williams & Wilkins.

Ministry of Community Safety and Correctional Services (MCSCS). (2015). *PREP. Fit to serve. Preparing for the PREP—The physical readiness evaluation for police.* Retrieved from http://www.applicanttesting.com/images/ stories/pdf/FittoServe2015Final.pdf

Ministry of Community Safety and Correctional Services (MCSCS). (2016). Careers in corrections. Retrieved from http://www.mcscs.jus.gov.on.ca/ english/corr_serv/careers_in_corr/careers_corr_about.html

Police Fitness Personnel of Ontario. (2017). Ontario police fitness standards. Retrived from http://pfpo.org

RCMP. (2013). *The RCMP PARE administrator manual and forms.* Ottawa: Author.

RunningWithUs. (n.d.). 5K Training Plans. Cancer Research UK RACE FOR LIFE. https://raceforlife.cancerresearchuk.org/prepare-for-your-event/ training-plans/5k

Seguin, R.A. (2015). Factors associated with success in PARE testing among RCMP officers. Electronic Thesis and Dissertation Repository. Retrieved from http://ir.lib.uwo.ca/etd/2856

Thompson, W.R., Gordon, N.F., Pescatello, L.S., American College of Sports Medicine, et al. (Eds.). (2010). ACSM's guidelines for exercise testing and prescription (8th ed.). Champaign, IL: Human Kinetics.

TRAINING LOGS

RECORD OF PERSONAL PHYSICAL TESTING RESULTS

RESISTANCE TRAINING WORKOUT LOG

CARDIOVASCULAR WORKOUT LOG

RECORD OF PERSONAL PHYSICAL TESTING RESULTS

	SEMESTER _____							
	Date:		**Date:**		**Date:**			
OPFA Components	**SCORE**		**SCORE**		**SCORE**			
Push-Ups	Number	/50	Time	/50	Time	/50		
Core Endurance	Time	/50	Level	/50	Level	/50		
Sit & Reach (Trunk Flexibility)	cm	/20	Number	/20	Number	/20		
1.5 mile Run	Time	/20	Time	/20	Time	/20		
20 m Shuttle Run	Stage	/10	cm	/10	cm	/10		
Total SCORE								
Strategies to improve my results								

BFOR	**To Be Successful**	**Date:**		**Date:**		**Date:**	
PREP	Pursuit Restraint Circuit <157 sec	Time		Time		Time	
	20 m Shuttle Run = 7.0	Stage		Stage		Stage	
FITCO	Search Station <120 sec	Time		Time		Time	
	Emergency Response Circuit <128 sec	Time		Time		Time	
	20 m Shuttle Run = 5.5	Stage		Stage		Stage	
PARE	Obstacle Course & Push/Pull CBS Officer <4:45 min RCMP Cadet <4:00 min	Time		Time		Time	
	Torso Bag Carry CBS Officer = 80 lbs RCMP Cadet = 100 lbs	Carry (wt)		Carry (wt)		Carry (wt)	
Strategies to improve my results							

Other Fitness Tests	**Date:**		**Date:**		**Date:**	
Chin-Ups	Number		Number		Number	
Bench Press	Weight		Weight		Weight	
Leg Press	Weight		Weight		Weight	
Strategies to improve my results						

RECORD OF PERSONAL PHYSICAL TESTING RESULTS

SEMESTER _____						
	Date:		Date:		Date:	
OPFA Components	SCORE		SCORE		SCORE	
Push-Ups	Number	/50	Time	/50	Time	/50
Core Endurance	Time	/50	Level	/50	Level	/50
Sit & Reach (Trunk Flexibility)	cm	/20	Number	/20	Number	/20
1.5 mile Run	Time	/20	Time	/20	Time	/20
20 m Shuttle Run	Stage	/10	cm	/10	cm	/10
Total SCORE						
Strategies to improve my results						

BFOR	To Be Successful	Date:		Date:		Date:	
PREP	Pursuit Restraint Circuit <157 sec	Time		Time		Time	
	20 m Shuttle Run = 7.0	Stage		Stage		Stage	
FITCO	Search Station <120 sec	Time		Time		Time	
	Emergency Response Circuit <128 sec	Time		Time		Time	
	20 m Shuttle Run = 5.5	Stage		Stage		Stage	
PARE	Obstacle Course & Push/Pull CBS Officer <4:45 min RCMP Cadet <4:00 min	Time		Time		Time	
	Torso Bag Carry CBS Officer = 80 lbs RCMP Cadet = 100 lbs	Carry (wt)		Carry (wt)		Carry (wt)	
Strategies to improve my results							

Other Fitness Tests	Date:		Date:		Date:	
Chin-Ups	Number		Number		Number	
Bench Press	Weight		Weight		Weight	
Leg Press	Weight		Weight		Weight	
Strategies to improve my results						

RECORD OF PERSONAL PHYSICAL TESTING RESULTS

SEMESTER _____						
	Date:		**Date:**		**Date:**	
OPFA Components	**SCORE**		**SCORE**		**SCORE**	
Push-Ups	Number	/50	Time	/50	Time	/50
Core Endurance	Time	/50	Level	/50	Level	/50
Sit & Reach (Trunk Flexibility)	cm	/20	Number	/20	Number	/20
1.5 mile Run	Time	/20	Time	/20	Time	/20
20 m Shuttle Run	Stage	/10	cm	/10	cm	/10
Total SCORE						
Strategies to improve my results						

BFOR	To Be Successful	Date:	Date:	Date:
PREP	Pursuit Restraint Circuit <157 sec	Time	Time	Time
	20 m Shuttle Run = 7.0	Stage	Stage	Stage
FITCO	Search Station <120 sec	Time	Time	Time
	Emergency Response Circuit <128 sec	Time	Time	Time
	20 m Shuttle Run = 5.5	Stage	Stage	Stage
PARE	Obstacle Course & Push/Pull CBS Officer <4:45 min RCMP Cadet <4:00 min	Time	Time	Time
	Torso Bag Carry CBS Officer = 80 lbs RCMP Cadet = 100 lbs	Carry (wt)	Carry (wt)	Carry (wt)
Strategies to improve my results				

Other Fitness Tests	Date:	Date:	Date:
Chin-Ups	Number	Number	Number
Bench Press	Weight	Weight	Weight
Leg Press	Weight	Weight	Weight
Strategies to improve my results			

RECORD OF PERSONAL PHYSICAL TESTING RESULTS

SEMESTER _____						
	Date:		Date:		Date:	
OPFA Components	**SCORE**		**SCORE**		**SCORE**	
Push-Ups	Number	/50	Time	/50	Time	/50
Core Endurance	Time	/50	Level	/50	Level	/50
Sit & Reach (Trunk Flexibility)	cm	/20	Number	/20	Number	/20
1.5 mile Run	Time	/20	Time	/20	Time	/20
20 m Shuttle Run	Stage	/10	cm	/10	cm	/10
Total SCORE						
Strategies to improve my results						

BFOR	**To Be Successful**	Date:		Date:		Date:	
PREP	Pursuit Restraint Circuit <157 sec	Time		Time		Time	
	20 m Shuttle Run = 7.0	Stage		Stage		Stage	
FITCO	Search Station <120 sec	Time		Time		Time	
	Emergency Response Circuit <128 sec	Time		Time		Time	
	20 m Shuttle Run = 5.5	Stage		Stage		Stage	
PARE	Obstacle Course & Push/Pull CBS Officer <4:45 min RCMP Cadet <4:00 min	Time		Time		Time	
	Torso Bag Carry CBS Officer = 80 lbs RCMP Cadet = 100 lbs	Carry (wt)		Carry (wt)		Carry (wt)	
Strategies to improve my results							

Other Fitness Tests	Date:		Date:		Date:	
Chin-Ups	Number		Number		Number	
Bench Press	Weight		Weight		Weight	
Leg Press	Weight		Weight		Weight	
Strategies to improve my results						

RESISTANCE TRAINING WORKOUT LOG

RESISTANCE WORKOUT LOG FOR:										DATE:
	Set 1		Set 2		Set 3		Set 4		Set 5	
Exercise	Weight	Reps	Weight	Reps	Weight	Reps	Weight	Reps	Weight	Reps

RESISTANCE WORKOUT LOG FOR:										DATE:
	Set 1		Set 2		Set 3		Set 4		Set 5	
Exercise	Weight	Reps	Weight	Reps	Weight	Reps	Weight	Reps	Weight	Reps

RESISTANCE TRAINING WORKOUT LOG

RESISTANCE WORKOUT LOG FOR:										DATE:
	Set 1		Set 2		Set 3		Set 4		Set 5	
Exercise	Weight	Reps	Weight	Reps	Weight	Reps	Weight	Reps	Weight	Reps

RESISTANCE WORKOUT LOG FOR:										DATE:
	Set 1		Set 2		Set 3		Set 4		Set 5	
Exercise	Weight	Reps	Weight	Reps	Weight	Reps	Weight	Reps	Weight	Reps

RESISTANCE TRAINING WORKOUT LOG

RESISTANCE WORKOUT LOG FOR:										DATE:	
	Set 1		Set 2		Set 3		Set 4		Set 5		
Exercise	Weight	Reps	Weight	Reps	Weight	Reps	Weight	Reps	Weight	Reps	

RESISTANCE WORKOUT LOG FOR:										DATE:	
	Set 1		Set 2		Set 3		Set 4		Set 5		
Exercise	Weight	Reps	Weight	Reps	Weight	Reps	Weight	Reps	Weight	Reps	

RESISTANCE TRAINING WORKOUT LOG

RESISTANCE WORKOUT LOG FOR:										DATE:
	Set 1		Set 2		Set 3		Set 4		Set 5	
Exercise	Weight	Reps	Weight	Reps	Weight	Reps	Weight	Reps	Weight	Reps

RESISTANCE WORKOUT LOG FOR:										DATE:
	Set 1		Set 2		Set 3		Set 4		Set 5	
Exercise	Weight	Reps	Weight	Reps	Weight	Reps	Weight	Reps	Weight	Reps

RESISTANCE TRAINING WORKOUT LOG

RESISTANCE WORKOUT LOG FOR:										DATE:
	Set 1		Set 2		Set 3		Set 4		Set 5	
Exercise	Weight	Reps	Weight	Reps	Weight	Reps	Weight	Reps	Weight	Reps

RESISTANCE WORKOUT LOG FOR:										DATE:
	Set 1		Set 2		Set 3		Set 4		Set 5	
Exercise	Weight	Reps	Weight	Reps	Weight	Reps	Weight	Reps	Weight	Reps

RESISTANCE TRAINING WORKOUT LOG

RESISTANCE WORKOUT LOG FOR:										DATE:
	Set 1		Set 2		Set 3		Set 4		Set 5	
Exercise	Weight	Reps	Weight	Reps	Weight	Reps	Weight	Reps	Weight	Reps

RESISTANCE WORKOUT LOG FOR:										DATE:
	Set 1		Set 2		Set 3		Set 4		Set 5	
Exercise	Weight	Reps	Weight	Reps	Weight	Reps	Weight	Reps	Weight	Reps

RESISTANCE TRAINING WORKOUT LOG

RESISTANCE WORKOUT LOG FOR:									DATE:	
	Set 1		Set 2		Set 3		Set 4		Set 5	
Exercise	Weight	Reps	Weight	Reps	Weight	Reps	Weight	Reps	Weight	Reps

RESISTANCE WORKOUT LOG FOR:									DATE:	
	Set 1		Set 2		Set 3		Set 4		Set 5	
Exercise	Weight	Reps	Weight	Reps	Weight	Reps	Weight	Reps	Weight	Reps

RESISTANCE TRAINING WORKOUT LOG

RESISTANCE WORKOUT LOG FOR:										DATE:
	Set 1		Set 2		Set 3		Set 4		Set 5	
Exercise	Weight	Reps	Weight	Reps	Weight	Reps	Weight	Reps	Weight	Reps

RESISTANCE WORKOUT LOG FOR:										DATE:
	Set 1		Set 2		Set 3		Set 4		Set 5	
Exercise	Weight	Reps	Weight	Reps	Weight	Reps	Weight	Reps	Weight	Reps

RESISTANCE TRAINING WORKOUT LOG

RESISTANCE WORKOUT LOG FOR:										DATE:
	Set 1		Set 2		Set 3		Set 4		Set 5	
Exercise	Weight	Reps	Weight	Reps	Weight	Reps	Weight	Reps	Weight	Reps

RESISTANCE WORKOUT LOG FOR:										DATE:
	Set 1		Set 2		Set 3		Set 4		Set 5	
Exercise	Weight	Reps	Weight	Reps	Weight	Reps	Weight	Reps	Weight	Reps

RESISTANCE TRAINING WORKOUT LOG

RESISTANCE WORKOUT LOG FOR:										DATE:
	Set 1		Set 2		Set 3		Set 4		Set 5	
Exercise	Weight	Reps	Weight	Reps	Weight	Reps	Weight	Reps	Weight	Reps

RESISTANCE WORKOUT LOG FOR:										DATE:
	Set 1		Set 2		Set 3		Set 4		Set 5	
Exercise	Weight	Reps	Weight	Reps	Weight	Reps	Weight	Reps	Weight	Reps

RESISTANCE TRAINING WORKOUT LOG

RESISTANCE WORKOUT LOG FOR:										DATE:
	Set 1		Set 2		Set 3		Set 4		Set 5	
Exercise	Weight	Reps	Weight	Reps	Weight	Reps	Weight	Reps	Weight	Reps

RESISTANCE WORKOUT LOG FOR:										DATE:
	Set 1		Set 2		Set 3		Set 4		Set 5	
Exercise	Weight	Reps	Weight	Reps	Weight	Reps	Weight	Reps	Weight	Reps

RESISTANCE TRAINING WORKOUT LOG

RESISTANCE WORKOUT LOG FOR:									DATE:	
	Set 1		Set 2		Set 3		Set 4		Set 5	
Exercise	Weight	Reps	Weight	Reps	Weight	Reps	Weight	Reps	Weight	Reps

RESISTANCE WORKOUT LOG FOR:									DATE:	
	Set 1		Set 2		Set 3		Set 4		Set 5	
Exercise	Weight	Reps	Weight	Reps	Weight	Reps	Weight	Reps	Weight	Reps

RESISTANCE TRAINING WORKOUT LOG

RESISTANCE WORKOUT LOG FOR:										DATE:
	Set 1		Set 2		Set 3		Set 4		Set 5	
Exercise	Weight	Reps	Weight	Reps	Weight	Reps	Weight	Reps	Weight	Reps

RESISTANCE WORKOUT LOG FOR:										DATE:
	Set 1		Set 2		Set 3		Set 4		Set 5	
Exercise	Weight	Reps	Weight	Reps	Weight	Reps	Weight	Reps	Weight	Reps

RESISTANCE TRAINING WORKOUT LOG

RESISTANCE WORKOUT LOG FOR:											DATE:
	Set 1		Set 2		Set 3		Set 4		Set 5		
Exercise	Weight	Reps	Weight	Reps	Weight	Reps	Weight	Reps	Weight	Reps	

RESISTANCE WORKOUT LOG FOR:											DATE:
	Set 1		Set 2		Set 3		Set 4		Set 5		
Exercise	Weight	Reps	Weight	Reps	Weight	Reps	Weight	Reps	Weight	Reps	

CARDIOVASCULAR WORKOUT LOG

Run, Shuttle Run, Interval Training		Semester				
Date	WORKOUT Type	Time hh:mm:ss	Distance kms/miles	Pace	HR	Temp (°C/°F)
		: :				
		: :				
		: :				
		: :				
		: :				
		: :				
		: :				
		: :				
		: :				
		: :				
		: :				
		: :				
		: :				
		: :				
		: :				
		: :				
		: :				
		: :				
		: :				
		: :				
		: :				
		: :				
		: :				
		: :				
		: :				
		: :				

CARDIOVASCULAR WORKOUT LOG

Run, Shuttle Run, Interval Training		Semester				
Date	WORKOUT Type	Time hh:mm:ss	Distance kms/miles	Pace	HR	Temp (°C/°F)
		: :				
		: :				
		: :				
		: :				
		: :				
		: :				
		: :				
		: :				
		: :				
		: :				
		: :				
		: :				
		: :				
		: :				
		: :				
		: :				
		: :				
		: :				
		: :				
		: :				
		: :				
		: :				
		: :				
		: :				
		: :				
		: :				
		: :				
		: :				
		: :				
		: :				

CARDIOVASCULAR WORKOUT LOG

Run, Shuttle Run, Interval Training		Semester				
Date	WORKOUT Type	Time hh:mm:ss	Distance kms/miles	Pace	HR	Temp (°C/°F)
		: :				
		: :				
		: :				
		: :				
		: :				
		: :				
		: :				
		: :				
		: :				
		: :				
		: :				
		: :				
		: :				
		: :				
		: :				
		: :				
		: :				
		: :				
		: :				
		: :				
		: :				
		: :				
		: :				
		: :				
		: :				
		: :				
		: :				

CARDIOVASCULAR WORKOUT LOG

Run, Shuttle Run, Interval Training		Semester				
Date	WORKOUT Type	Time hh:mm:ss	Distance kms/miles	Pace	HR	Temp (°C/°F)
		: :				
		: :				
		: :				
		: :				
		: :				
		: :				
		: :				
		: :				
		: :				
		: :				
		: :				
		: :				
		: :				
		: :				
		: :				
		: :				
		: :				
		: :				
		: :				
		: :				
		: :				
		: :				
		: :				
		: :				
		: :				
		: :				
		: :				
		: :				
		: :				

CREDITS

All photos of exercises taken by Heather Gough and Nancy Wisotzki.

Page 5 (FITCO Performance Components): Reproduced from Becoming a Correctional Services Officer: FITCO - Fitness Test for Ontario Correctional Officer Applicants, 2016 (URL: https://www.mcscs.jus.gov.on.ca/english/corr _serv/careers_in_corr/become_corr_off/FITCO/cs_FITCO.html). © Queen's Printer for Ontario, 2016. Reproduced with permission.

Page 15: Canadian Forces Morale and Welfare Services, 2016. Reproduced with permission.

Page 16: Canadian Forces Morale and Welfare Services, 2016. Reproduced with permission.

Page 17: Canadian Forces Morale and Welfare Services, 2016. Reproduced with permission.

Page 125: Reprinted with the permission of Police Fitness Personnel of Ontario.

Page 129: Reprinted with the permission of Police Fitness Personnel of Ontario.

Page 132: Reprinted with the permission of Police Fitness Personnel of Ontario.

Page 134: Reprinted with the permission of Police Fitness Personnel of Ontario.

Page 136: Reprinted with the permission of Police Fitness Personnel of Ontario.

Page 138: ADAPTED with permission. Marian Reeves. Peel Regional Police Service 2017recruit standards. 2017 Brampton, Ontario, Peel Regional Police.

Page 139: ADAPTED with permission. Marian Reeves. Peel Regional Police Service 2017recruit standards. 2017 Brampton, Ontario, Peel Regional Police.

Page 143: ADAPTED with permission. Marian Reeves. Peel Regional Police Service 2017recruit standards. 2017 Brampton, Ontario, Peel Regional Police.